"What a practical guide to relationships! *Pollyanna goes beyond the whimsical notion of manifestation and actually hands us the tools to create the relationship of our dreams. Not only is* The Relationship Revelation *a manual for love, these active lessons will be applicable to every aspect of life. Thank you for simplifying a challenging topic and sharing your simple strategies.*"

KATE NUTT, photographer

"*This book really is a revelation! Pollyanna Darling has done a marvelous job of making it clear that we are the sole determinant of what we create. The beauty of her premise is that the consciousness she evokes to attract the love we yearn for can equally be applied to creating everything else that matters to us.*"

WILLIAM WHITECLOUD, author of The Magician's Way

"*With refreshing directness and candor Pollyanna Darling challenges us to look at, and own, the self-defeating stories we carry in relationships. She offers us a method, through intuition, to step beyond these stories and create the relationships and life that we truly love. There's nowhere to hide. Slap yourself in the face by reading and trying the processes in this book. (There will be no need to come and see me)!*"

TIM LOUGHNAN, psychologist and family therapist

"The Relationship Revelation *is special. It is clear, logical and gets right to the heart of the matter: 'It's All You'. By focusing on what you want to create in life, the book gives back the power to manifest without the limitations created by old patterns. I only wish this book had been around many years ago, it would have saved me a lot of heartache.*"

DR ARNE RUBINSTEIN (MBBS, FRACGP),
CEO The Australian Rites of Passage Institute

"*Pollyanna Darling's new book* The Relationship Revelation *is an important book for our times. There are far too many proscriptive texts out there and we have an over supply of 'experts'. Pollyanna with her highly attuned intuitive skills and training, brings to the market a powerful new methodology for exploring relationships.*"

MORRIS KAPLAN, author, journalist and publisher

"*Oh my god, I've been going out with myself all the time. No wonder it was always such a disappointment! In order to improve my relationships, I had to improve myself. I could have done without that self knowledge. You know it was so much easier when I could sit back and blame men for all their inadequacies without having to even contemplate mine!*"

MANDY NOLAN, comedian and serial monogamist

"*This is a book for those brave souls who are ready to step outside the usual toxic, regressive paradigm and actually dare to create fulfilling, passionate and alive relationships! There is so much nonsense out there about relationships and most of it misses the fundamental point. I found Pollyanna's book beautifully clear, easy to relate to, and fun to read. The message is profound but so simple. Try it on, and it could change not only your relationships, but your whole life!*"

MAYA STANGE, actress

"*Pollyanna has completely changed the way I look at relationships. If you thought you knew what being a partner was all about, this book will show you there's a whole lot more to being with somebody than just turning up and saying I love you every now and then.*"

MATT GRANFIELD, author and journalist

THE RELATIONSHIP REVELATION

It's All You

THE RELATIONSHIP REVELATION

It's All You

by

POLLYANNA DARLING

IMAGINARIA

First published in Australia in 2011
by Imaginaria
PO Box 405
Brunswick Heads NSW 2482

www.imaginariabooks.com

"Creator Alignment Process" reprinted with the kind permission
of William Whitecloud – www.williamwhitecloud.com

National Library of Australia Cataloguing-in-Publication entry:

Author: Darling, Pollyanna.

Title: The relationship revelation : it's all you / by Pollyanna
Darling.

ISBN: 9780987116406 (pbk.)

Subjects: Interpersonal relations.

Dewey Number: 158.2

Cover photography and graphic design: Cathy Martin Creative
Design – www.cathymartincreative.com

Editing, Book Design and Typesetting: Laurel Cohn Editing and
Manuscript Development Services – www.laurelcohn.com.au

Printed by Lightning Source on PEFC paper

Acknowledgments

A big thank you to all the people who have encouraged and supported me in writing this book, there are many of you and I appreciate every single one. A special thank you to those of you who shared your stories with me and gave me feedback and to The Magician's Way Foundation for your support.

My heartfelt appreciation, gratitude and love goes to my patient, wonderful partner and king, Asher. Without his encouragement, assistance and love, I wouldn't have begun, never mind completed, this book!

And finally, to my four beautiful children, thank you for your patience and deliciously innocent words of support (and sometimes frustration). One day you will all have relationships – may they be everything you dream of.

Contents

A Quick Word   *13*

♯ PART 1

It's All You   *17*

What is a Relationship?   *19*
It's All You   *20*
Creative Consciousness   *23*

♯ PART 2

The Underlying Assumption   *29*

Creating Crap   *31*
Tension   *33*
Underlying Assumptions   *37*
Formation of Assumptions   *40*
In Summary   *48*
Practical Steps Towards Transformation   *49*

Identifying Your Underlying Assumptions   *51*

The Role of Thoughts and Emotions   *54*
Noticing Your Body   *57*
Practical Steps Towards Transformation   *58*

Shifting the Power   *61*

Temptation   *62*
Being Guided by Feelings   *64*
In Summary   *66*

Awareness of Your Addictions 67
Emotional Freedom 70
Incompleteness 72
In Summary 74

PART 3

Common Relationship Dynamics Dynamited 75

Collusion 77
Fighting 80
Practical Conflict 82
It Means Nothing 83
Know Thyself 85
The Right Stuff 88
Violence in Relationships 89
Pain 91
Boring Old Blame 92
In Summary 95

PART 4

Creating The Relationship of Your Dreams 97

What Would You Love? 99
Shifting Your Focus 101
Discovering What You Would Truly Love 103
Meet Your Soul Partner Meditation 104
Using Your Intuition to Discover Your Truth 106
The Relationship of Your Dreams 110
Tips for Using Your Intuition 111

Resolving Tension   117
Hanging Out in the Unknown   118
The Power of Choice   119
Taking Action   122
Acting in Favour of Your Creation   124
Force Versus Focus   127
Using Choice   128
Owning Your Desires   129
The Far Horizon Trap   131
Practical Choice   132

Imagination and Receiving   134

Your Imagination Amplifies Your Focus   134
Practical Imagination   135
Receiving Your Creation   136
Timing   140
Practical Receiving   141

PART 5

Transforming Your Existing Relationship   143

Your Current Relationship Reality   146
Tall Tales   151
Defining Reality   153
Shifting the Focus to What You Love   156
The Truth About Your Partner   157
Your True Nature and Expanded Essence   159
Your Partner's True Nature and Expanded Essence 162
Truth and Definition   164
Happily Ever After   165

Create or Surrender	166
Vulnerability	168
Forget Perfect	168
Know Yourself (here it is again!!)	170
Practical Relationship Transformation	171
Children	172
Beware the Stories	175
Weaving Children into Your Creation	177
In Summary	178

PART 6

Sex, Lovemaking and Myth	179
Sex and the Limited Self	181
Lovemaking From Your Infinite Creative Being	182
Practical Sexual Magic	184
Creating Myth	185
Now Create It	188

PART 7

Resources		189
i	Other Ways To Use This Book	191
ii	Soul Partner Guided Meditation	194
iii	Creator Alignment Process (modified)	197
iv	Thoughts, Emotions and Assumptions	201
v	Books and Trainings	210

A Quick Word

I want to be direct right from the outset – no waffle.

You may have met those conscious types who tell you that the truly enlightened have no need for an intimate relationship. Maybe it's true. You won't find that here. I love life and everything it has to offer, including the possibility of enjoying a loving, sexual, intimate, joyous, deeply connected relationship with another human being.

For those of us who relish the touch of another, the pleasure of love-making, the sharing of life's rampant journey, establishing and then continuing a joyful connection with another human is a very satisfying part of life.

If you would love to create intimacy, love, companionship, sharing and all the other wonderful (and sometimes not so wonderful) things that come with a relationship, you are in the right place.

If you would love to transform your existing intimate relationship into a magical journey with your soul mate, you are in the right place.

The relationship you would love to create is within your grasp and if you give yourself over to what lies in these pages, you WILL create it, and much sooner than you think.

If you want a relationship with another human so that you can feel wanted, to fill in the emptiness, to give purpose to your life or to complete you in some way, you may as well pop this book right back up there on the shelf, it's not for you!

This book is an exploration, a guide and a celebration of the joy that's available to us, expressed through an intimate relationship.

You may be familiar with many of the concepts and happy to accept them. You may find the whole thing completely ludicrous. I'm happy to assure you that if you implement the strategies in this book, whether you think they're the bees knees or a crock of crap, you will create more magic in your relationships than you would ever have believed possible.

The basic principles of this book can be found in the core philosophy of many of the major religions of the world in one form or another. They are primarily taken from Hermetic Philosophy, a body of works that is said to have emerged around

200 BCE from Alexandrian Egypt. This philosophy is based on the teachings of a figure known as Hermes Trismegistus. Some of these teachings formed the philosophy of the Gnostic tradition of early Christianity. It is not necessary to have read (or even heard of) the philosophy in order to create the relationship you would love, but if you would like to investigate further, feel free to check out the references included at the end of this book.

This is not a Christian book and takes no religious context or moral position.

This book will never require you to fix yourself or your partner, 'work on' yourself or anyone else, or change yourself.

This is not, and does not pretend to be, a psychology book. It is purely and simply a guide, that if followed and acted upon, will facilitate the creation of the relationship you would love.

The fundamental structure of this book hinges on a model presented in Part 1. The book also contains a number of premises which support the model and will radically change your reality. You are not required to believe the model or any of the premises that support it, it makes no difference to the end result.

If you want to create a truly wonderful relationship for yourself and get the most out of this book, all you need to do is assume that the model and the premises supporting it are true. Act as if they are true, think about them as though they were true. See what happens. Experiment with them in your life, check out the results, experiment a little more. As you come across each premise, you will have a response or perhaps a reaction, let that be there and just allow yourself to work with each one.

This book also contains a number of relationship stories that illustrate the model. All these stories are from real people who were kind enough to share their experiences with absolute honesty.

Included with this book are several audio files to assist you with the intuitive exercises presented in Part 4. These audio files are available to download from my website. Full details are provided in the text at the appropriate moments.

So, without any further preamble, let's get on with it. Have a wonderful journey!

PART 1

It's All You

What is a Relationship?

Everyone is either in one, wants one or doesn't want one. We talk about relationships and their problems incessantly, they can make your life miserable or wonderful, great rafts of people search the Internet every day for help with them, but what actually is a relationship?

You can't see it, you can't smell it, you can't touch it, you can't taste it – it's not tangible. It's not real. A relationship is an imaginary concept. When you are telling yourself or others that your relationship is dysfunctional or that it's wonderful, you are talking about a phantom. When you are yearning and longing to have a relationship, you are pining after something that isn't real! When you are investing your energy in trying to improve your relationship, or talking to your partner about how to improve your relationship, you are focusing on something that doesn't actually exist. It's weird when you think about it.

Of course, your partner (or the partner you would like) does exist, but the relationship is created by you in your imagination. The relationship you *have* and the relationship you *want* are only limited by the scope of your imagination.

It's All You

Your relationship is made up by you, in your imagination. Which brings me to the model that this whole book is based on, the revelation referred to in the title: *It's All You.*

> You are entirely responsible for everything that takes place in your relationship.

Every moment of your existence is a creation, every minute of every hour of every day, you are creating, whether you are aware of it or not. This applies to your relationship too. You are the creator, you are doing all of it. Every action you take, every word that you say (or don't say), every gesture, etc., is an action/gesture/word in favour of *something*.

It's All You – you are creating your relationship as you live it.

Often when I explain this model, people say, *"Oh, so you mean I'm seeing it all from my perspective, it's my experience?"* No, that's not what I mean.

The model shows that you are actually *creating* everything that occurs in your relationship. Of course you are also experiencing those creations from your perspective, but no one is doing anything *to* you, you are generating the reality you experience.

I'm introducing this now because it's the most important concept in this book, it's the model from which you will create the relationship of your dreams. If you can get your mind, body and soul around this one, you will totally transform your relationships with other human beings – all of them, not just your relationship with your partner.

In the course of my coaching work, I so often hear:

"Well, it's my partner's pattern to behave in this way."

"She's doing this to me."

"We're co-creating, blah blah blah."

Nonsense! Everything that takes place in your relationship is being created by you whether you are aware of it or not. *It's All You.*

Having said that, for the vast majority of us (including me), much of what we create in our intimate relationships is done unconsciously, without awareness.

We're simply not aware of what we are focused on, of the structures we have unconsciously set up and the havoc that this focus can wreak in our lives.

Hang in here with me and continue the journey of this book to the very end and you will be a long way towards understanding what your unconscious relationship dynamics are. You will also be in a much better position to create a relationship that you will truly love.

I also introduce this concept right up the front, because it's probably the most difficult to swallow.

What? All those beastly, horrid, misery-making, uncomfortable, humiliating, unpleasant and rotten things that have taken place in my relationships are *my* doing? Little old me, minding my own business, I did that? I don't believe it. Surely it's partly his/her fault, surely it's because of my circumstances or the way I/my partner was raised? It can't all be me, why would I do that to myself? And so on.

Just the idea of your own role as the creator may generate anger, sadness, depression, blame and any number of other emotions in you. That's fine, let those emotions be there and keep reading.

Remember too, that the awesome, beautiful, amazing and sacred moments in your relationships were also created by you.

> You don't need to believe in the model. Suspend all of that for the time being and allow this one to rest in your consciousness. Let it hang about there and keep it in mind while you read on.

Creative Consciousness

So how is it possible that you are doing all of it? Contrary to what you might think, you are not a victim of your circumstances, your partner, your family, your friends, your obnoxious neighbour, global warming, peak oil, and so on. You are not a victim at all.

You are a divinely creative consciousness in a physical body, here to live and create the life you love. You have a raft of natural talents and abilities that support you in creating this life and you have an innate, easily accessible ability to create, transform and maintain an intimate relationship that will nourish and elate you.

> It's a premise –
> you are a divinely creative being.

You don't need to believe it, just assume it's true. You are a divinely creative being, you are connected to all things and you have a consciousness capable of creating everything that you would love. You are here in this life to express your true nature, to create what you would truly love to see and experience in the world.

As this divinely creative being, you have an infinitely powerful consciousness. This power can be used to generate the true desires of your infinite being, or to generate the murky realities of your unconscious beliefs. It's up to you.

Imagine for a moment the creative power of such a consciousness – there is nothing it's not aware of. The power of this expanded, extraordinary consciousness can be focused on anything, create anything.

Imagine it as a supercharged searchlight on a lighthouse with a view of everything. Wherever and whatever the searchlight lands on generates your reality. Until you become aware of the power of this light, it is just swinging about in the darkness, randomly falling on things, randomly creating your reality – sometimes focused on what you want, sometimes on what you don't want.

Once you acknowledge your own power and experience it for yourself, you become the lighthouse keeper. You can guide the light to the places you want it to go and create everything that you love, including an amazing relationship.

Once again: every moment of your existence is a creation, you are the creator. You are incredibly powerful. The good, the bad, the ugly and the beautiful moments of your life are all generated from within that consciousness. Your consciousness is creating your relationships, your family, your environment, your workplace, your friends, your health, your garden, your entire experience.

All the major religions, myths and heroes journeys directly or indirectly point to this premise that you are a divinely creative being. When you live your life assuming that this premise is true, the most magical and extraordinary things happen.

There is nothing that stands in the way of you creating what you would love, including a relationship with another human that is fulfilling, engaging, fun, loving, passionate, whatever your heart truly desires, regardless of your circumstances.

To whet your appetite for the model *It's All You* and the premise that you are a divinely creative being, check out the real-life story below.

I don't want your children ...

Tammy and Jason had only recently started seeing each other when little cracks started showing in the relationship. Tammy had been divorced for a couple of years and had two children. Jason, an artist in his late thirties, had never married and had no children of his own.

They met in a very romantic and magical way and fell in love. Tammy managed to arrange her life so that she had plenty of time to spend with Jason without the kids.

Inevitably, as they spent more time with each other, Jason came into contact with Tammy's children more frequently. He liked them, but wasn't keen to spend lots of time with them. After about three months, he began requesting that Tammy go out with him alone, that she find someone to look after the children. He made it clear that their presence was a problem for him and complained often about it.

Tammy wasn't happy. She loved her children and wanted a man who would embrace them. She was also crazy about Jason. She became more and more concerned about the situation and was experiencing the terrible tension of being torn between her kids and her man.

She was miserable and on the verge of ending the relationship, despite her passion for Jason. They were bickering and sniping at each other – things were going downhill rapidly.

At that point, we did an exercise (described in Part 7 (iii), page 197) to shift the power of Tammy's infinitely powerful creative consciousness out of her limited, victim mentality and into what she would love to create – which was to be with a loving, beautiful man who would embrace her children and be part of a loving family with her.

Almost unbelievably, the very next day, Jason asked Tammy out to a barbecue and said they should all go as a family. He started playing with the children and, to Tammy's amazement, she even caught him leaping around laughing on the trampoline with them.

Jason and Tammy are happily married now and have a child of their own.

It is worth pointing out that Tammy never discussed Jason's attitude with him. There were no conversations about the problem. They didn't try to 'work it out'. From the time that Tammy did the exercise to shift the power, not one word was said to Jason. I didn't do any work with him and nor did anyone else.

> His behaviour changed completely overnight in the most extraordinary way, simply because Tammy stopped focusing on her crappy, unconscious assumptions and put the power of her infinite consciousness into what she would love to create.

Enough said about that for now. There are numerous examples in this book which illustrate the truth of the premise that you are a divinely creative being with an infinitely powerful consciousness, but you don't need to believe it. Just have a go at acting as if it were true and keep reading.

> "Man is an exception, whatever else he is. If he is not the image of God, then he is a disease of the dust. If it is not true that a divine being fell, then we can only say that one of the animals went entirely off its head."
>
> GK Chesterton

PART 2

The Underlying Assumption

Creating Crap

Okay, so if you're this amazing, infinite being, you may be asking yourself, *"How come I keep creating crappy partners and unfulfilling relationships that end in miserable breakups? Why am I not creating spectacularly sexy, fulfilling and awesome relationships with deliriously wonderful partners?"*

They're good questions and there's a good answer. From the moment you arrived as a consciousness in your mother's womb, ready to have an individual experience of life, you have been conditioned into believing that you are limited by your own talents, knowledge and abilities (or lack of them), by your mind, by those around you, by your circumstances and ultimately, by the world 'out there'.

Your experiences in childhood convince you that you are a limited being with limited potential and possibilities – your limited self. This is variously referred to as 'ego', 'personality', 'identity' etc. It's a cut-down, bargain bin version of your true self which, left to its own devices, always creates a reality that you will find unpleasant. It's like having a deranged monkey in charge of your searchlight, flashing it about without a care for where it lands.

In your limited self you also have pinched and limited ideas about what's possible from/with others and the world. You have an idea about what 'reality' is and you go about your daily life behaving as though the limits you have imagined actually exist.

In my own case, I repeatedly settled for relationships and partners that were less than what I wanted because I didn't believe that the relationship I truly wanted was possible. In fact, I thought that my desire to have a deeply romantic, sexy, fulfilling relationship was ridiculous and silly. I would never have told anyone about it for fear of being mocked. Consequently, I never went for it, I never tried to create it. I just sort of quietly hoped that it might happen. It didn't.

Of course, now I am living in a totally different reality where my dreams are always within reach. I am living the relationship I always secretly wanted. So can you. I'll explain later how to create it, but in the meantime it's important to recognise and understand how you have created (or perhaps haven't created) your relationships up to now.

Generally speaking, with the monkey in charge of the searchlight, you will chart a rocky path through your adult life, sometimes in light, sometimes in darkness. You will repeat the same tired old patterns and situations over and over again, especially in your intimate relationships. While the power of your infinite consciousness is bound up in the preoccupations of your limited self, your dream relationship will remain out of your reach.

Tension

Understanding tension and its different forms will greatly assist you in understanding yourself and the ways that you create, especially in your relationships. Tension comes in two main forms: psychological and structural.

As a human being, you experience tension. You may be highly aware of it, you may not be aware of it at all.

> Tension always demands resolution.
> That's another premise. One way or another,
> the tension must be resolved.

Psychological Tension

Imagine your partner has a very irritating habit – he/she is forever leaving the butter out of the fridge. It melts and when you have your toast, it's rancid. This is very aggravating for you and you experience tension (in your mind, your body and/ or your emotional state). That tension demands that you resolve it. The most common way would be to say something to your partner about the irritating habit, such as:

"How come you're always leaving the butter out?"

Or, *"It's really annoying that you always leave the butter out."*

Or, *"I'm so fed up with the way you always leave the butter out."*

Or even (for advanced souls, but still resolving tension): *"I'd really appreciate it if you would put the butter away after you use it."*

This in turn would create psychological tension for your partner. He/she may ignore it and put the butter away, or he/she may resolve the tension by griping at you about something. You may become more annoyed and your levels of tension would balloon out, screaming at you to resolve, resolve, resolve:

"DO SOMETHING ABOUT IT".

Before you know it, you are in a full blown argument with mudslinging, swearing and shouting. After the argument you experience even deeper psychological tension because of the way your partner behaved. You imagine that your relationship is in trouble. How can you be with someone who treats you like this? What are you doing? And so on. These thoughts create more tension demanding resolution.

You might now initiate conversations with your partner about how the relationship can be fixed, how his/her behaviour makes you feel and so on. It may not go the way you wanted, generating yet more tension. And on it goes, until eventually you resolve your tension by ending the relationship.

This may not be how *you* go about things, but you can see how psychological tension leads inevitably to more and more tension needing resolution. And it all started because the butter got left out on the table!

One of the first steps in creating a relationship you will love is to begin to notice your relationship with psychological tension. You may notice this tension in your body, in your mind (your thoughts), in your emotions and in the things you want to say. If you have a partner, you will find many occasions to notice your tension! If you do not have a partner, just notice how tension arises in your interactions with others (family are especially good for this).

Notice how you want to behave when you are experiencing tension. Don't worry about doing anything about it, just notice for now.

Structural Tension

Structural tension refers to the state where what you want to create is markedly different to the reality you are currently experiencing.

Imagine a rubber band stretched between two little posts – this is a structure. As you move the posts apart, the elastic band becomes taut – a tension is created. If you keep moving the posts apart, eventually that tension will be resolved by the elastic band breaking or pinging off around the room. This will always happen with this structure.

The same is true of any structure – if you work with it, it will have a reliable outcome. If you change the structure, you will get a different outcome.

> *"Once you establish structural tension, your natural tendency will be to generate actions in order to resolve the tension"*.
>
> Robert Fritz

What on earth does this have to do with your relationship, I hear you ask?

Well, the underlying structures in your consciousness will dictate the nature of your relationship.

You can consciously use a structure that will always result in a relationship you love, or you can create from the structures that already exist in your unconscious mind. These generally result in relationships that are unsatisfactory.

With the help of this book, you will learn about your underlying structures and the tensions created by them. You will also learn how to generate a structure that will propel you towards the relationship you would truly love, using structural tension.

Underlying Assumptions

Perhaps you are reading this book because you want to create an amazing relationship, or you want to transform your existing relationship into the one of your dreams. Perhaps you are just curious! If you don't have the relationship of your wildest dreams, the power of your consciousness is not invested where it needs to be. You do not have a structure in place to create what you would love.

So where is this power actually invested?

It's in your underlying assumptions. Your underlying assumptions are the reason you don't create the relationship you would love, the reason you don't sustain the relationship you would love and the cause of all of the problems in your relationship. Underlying assumptions are the worm in the apple, the stone in the jam, the cat among the pigeons, the pirates in the deep blue sea.

Understanding and outing your underlying assumptions is at the heart of this book! They are underlying because until you out them, these assumptions reside in your unconscious (that which you are not consciously aware of). *You don't know about them!*

> Assume: take upon oneself,
> simulate, take for granted.

Your underlying assumptions are what you believe are truths about yourself, others and the world. You take it for granted that they are absolute truth and generally you are not aware of them. They are often irrational and make no sense at all to an outside observer.

For example, a person who appears to have a great deal of power in the world, such as a director of a huge business or a high level politician, could have a strong underlying assumption that they are powerless. This assumption drives them to acquire positions with perceived power to try and alleviate the psychological tension generated by the assumption of powerlessness.

Have a look at the collection of assumptions below (from real people). You may have one, some or even all of them:

- I'm unworthy of love
- I'm not good enough
- I can't have what I want
- I don't belong

- I need to control myself, others and the world
- I'm unlovable
- I'm not safe
- I'm powerless
- I need to be perfect
- I'm going to be rejected
- I'm not important
- I'm going to be let down
- There's a way the world is
- I don't trust others and they won't like me or love me
- I'd better be good or something bad will happen
- I can't make the right decision, I can't trust myself
- Others can have it, but I can't
- What I love isn't mine
- I'm bad and I make men do bad things
- I shouldn't desire the things I desire, I shouldn't expect to get them – I can't have what I want

My children and I call these assumptions our 'bags' – they're made of paper, you pull them over your head and suddenly you stop seeing things as they really are. Everything is coloured by whatever your 'bag' happens to be: I can't, it's not fair, I can't trust others, I'm insignificant, etc.

Identifying and understanding your underlying assumptions is critical to creating a flourishing relationship. *Nothing* generates an unsatisfying reality like having your searchlight firmly focused on your underlying assumptions.

Judgement

Just to add to your woes, the searchlight isn't discerning, it has no clue what is in your best interests or what would be enjoyable for you to experience. *It's just trained on whatever has the power.* It could be a shipload of pirates, the searchlight doesn't care.

Your infinite creative being says *"Ooh pirates have the power this month, that's fun!"* And before you know it, your reality is full of painful swashbuckling and your relationship stinks.

If you take the power of your consciousness out of your underlying assumptions and put it into creating the relationship you would love, you *will* create the relationship of your dreams.

Formation of Assumptions

Assumptions that do not serve you were formed in early childhood and then proven throughout the rest of your life. They are what you made up as a child when you experienced the pain of not having your needs fully met.

They are the servants of your limited self. They create needless misery and circumstances that you will not truly enjoy.

Your underlying assumptions cannot be changed. That's right, for better or worse, you will always have major and minor underlying assumptions hanging about in your consciousness. They will arise every time you go to create and are especially rampant in your intimate relationships.

So don't even think about trying to change them or get rid of them, or (as some self-help modalities suggest) work on them. It's a complete waste of your time and energy.

Plus, any time you are attempting to eliminate or change an underlying assumption, you are putting all the power of your consciousness in that assumption. Pointless!

Happily, if you take the focus of your infinite consciousness off your underlying assumptions and invest it in what you would truly love, you will be amazed at the marvellous relationship you can create.

You will learn to live with the voice of your underlying assumptions once you have identified them. You will come to view that voice as a rather deranged friend who is trying to protect you – well-meaning, but with completely the wrong idea!

Once you have identified your major assumptions, you will look back through your life and see how many incidents, behaviours and circumstances have their roots in those assumptions.

Your assumptions were formed in early childhood; they have nothing to do with now, yet they have tremendous power in your intimate relationships. It's as though the lighthouse is running really old software – remember the Commodore 64 and trying to do everything in DOS? Maybe you do, maybe you don't, but you wouldn't try to run the first version of Windows on your iPhone. Your phone would become entirely dysfunctional! None of the apps would work.

This is what happens in your relationship when you have the power of your consciousness invested in your underlying assumptions – none of your apps work!

As a child, it's your parents who supply you with validation, who are the unwitting players in the formation of your underlying assumptions. In adulthood, you unconsciously seek a parental substitute who will continue to validate (or not) your needs, and you invest all your energy in the most eligible candidate – your partner.

If you don't have a partner, you will have another parental-substitute relationship – your flatmate, your close friend, your brother/sister, the government (yes this happens), your dog!

I'm sure you've heard people talking about turning their partners into their mothers or fathers, or having 'mother stuff' or 'father stuff' with their partners. It's simply the result of unresolved pain from childhood, which truthfully can *never* be resolved, because it was made up in the first place.

Each time an event took place in your childhood where your needs went unmet, you experienced pain and tension. You asked, *"Why am I feeling pain?"* Then, to resolve the tension, you simply made up the answer (your underlying assumption) and stashed it in your unconscious mind.

Here is a real-life example of the formation of an assumption which then generates a reality in adult life:

Childhood Event
Elizabeth (aged 2) needs to tell her dad something. He's sitting in a wing-back chair. He's angry and dismissive. He tells her to go away. She feels unhappy.

Childhood Story (what she made up at age 2 in that experience)
Daddy doesn't care about me.

Underlying Assumption (carried into adulthood)
I'm not important.

Current Problem in Relationship
Constantly fighting with her partner.

Elizabeth experienced pain because her father was angry and told her to go away. That pain created a tension in her that screamed out to be resolved. So she would have asked herself, why am I in pain? Her unconscious mind came up with a reason *"I'm not important."*

Before and after this experience, there would have been other similar experiences where that unconscious assumption of not being important would be confirmed over and over again.

In her adult life Elizabeth is constantly trying to resolve the terrible tension that the assumption is creating by testing her partner to see if she's important to him. Because the power of her consciousness is invested in the assumption, she continuously creates a reality where her partner proves to her how unimportant she is.

As a result, they fight continuously. Elizabeth is not aware that the assumption is creating this reality. She is only aware of the constant conflict with her partner.

Here's another real-life example:

Childhood Event
Mark (aged 4 months) is alone in a cot at his aunty and uncle's house. He knows his mum is at home crying. He feels totally rejected, totally unloved. He's alone in the room and feels that his heart is collapsing.

Childhood Story (what he made up at 4 months old in that experience)
People don't care about me and I have to do everything myself.

Underlying Assumption (carried into adulthood)
I'm unlovable and unwanted.

Current Problem in Relationship
Keep going out with women who are geographically far away.

In this example, the pain and subsequent tension of Mark's lonely experience at four months led him to form the assumption that he's unlovable. Other incidents in his childhood would have reinforced this assumption.

With the power of his infinite consciousness focused on this assumption, he keeps creating a reality where he only has relationships with women who live a long way away, or who suddenly move away as soon as the relationship gets interesting. He then continues the relationship from a distance, wondering what to do about it and feeling unsatisfied and disappointed. Most of the time he's alone.

The tension created by Mark's underlying assumption that he is unlovable drives him to create relationships that are far from what he would love. Those relationships end up proving his original assumption.

Basically, it's a set up. You might, for example, believe you're unlovable so you continually set up relationships that prove it. It looks something like this:

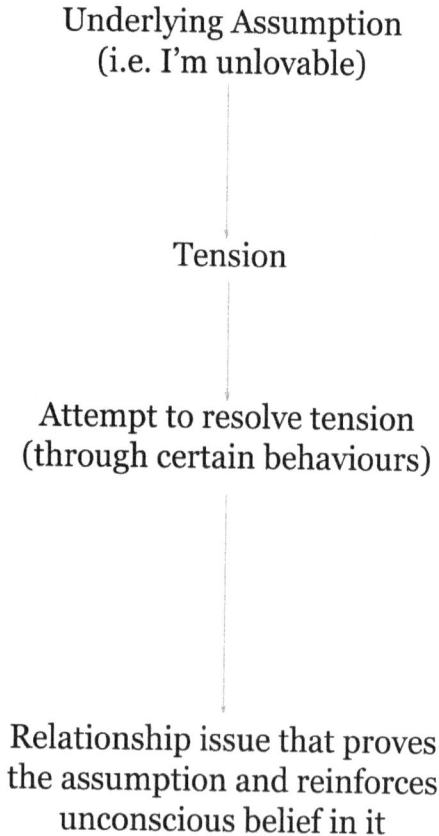

Underlying Assumption
(i.e. I'm unlovable)

Tension

Attempt to resolve tension
(through certain behaviours)

Relationship issue that proves
the assumption and reinforces
unconscious belief in it

These assumptions are buried in your unconscious mind until you out them. You don't know that you are focused on them. Mark was not aware that he was focused on being unlovable and unwanted, but his searchlight was fully trained on that belief and he continuously generated similar relationship scenarios. This can be very frustrating!

Here's one more real-life example of the formation of an underlying assumption, based on a childhood event:

Childhood Event
Angela (aged 3) is just out of sight, witnessing her parents arguing. She thinks her mother feels really hard done by and is unacknowledged. She's frightened but thinks it's better when they argue verbally because sometimes it gets violent. She feels alone and unsafe.

Childhood Story (what she made up at 3 in that experience)
That it's safer to keep the verbal fight alive.

Underlying Assumption (carried into adulthood)
It's not safe when I'm relating with men.

Current Problem in Relationship
Keep hooking into petty fighting in the relationship.

In this example, you can see that Angela's childhood fear of parental arguments turning violent and her identification with her mother, led her to form the assumption that she's not safe when relating with men. This in turn means that in her adult reality, she unconsciously feels safe when she's engaged in verbal spats with her partner.

Your searchlight is not discerning. Whatever it is trained on, wherever the power of your consciousness is invested, is created, whether it makes sense to a rational mind or not.

In Summary

You are a powerful being, the creator of your experience.

You can create unconsciously or consciously – either way, you are constantly creating.

Your unsatisfying and 'failed' creations are driven by your underlying assumptions, regardless of what they are.

There is no judgement in your infinite being about *what* your underlying assumptions are, it doesn't care if they are crap and will make you miserable.

Practical Steps Towards Transformation

Enough with the theory! What can you do to start creating the relationship you would love?

Step 1

Assume that the model *It's All You* is true. Act as if it is. Notice the results.

Step 2

Begin to notice how you deal with tension.

If you are not currently in a relationship, notice how you deal with tension in your life and with other people.

Be aware of when you are in psychological tension and ask yourself: What am I thinking? What am I feeling? Write it down if it helps.

If you are in a relationship, begin to notice when you experience tension. Forget about any thoughts you are having about how it's your partner's fault. Let him/her rant and rave (if that's what they're doing!) and bring your awareness back to yourself.

Ask yourself: what am I thinking and feeling? What triggered this tension in me? Write it down if it'll help you remember.

Be especially aware of your inner experience when you are in open conflict with your partner. Conflict is a great place for observing and learning about yourself. If the conflict is too heated and you are consumed by it, don't worry. Review it later by yourself and reflect on the questions above.

In either case, be particularly aware of any ways in which you resolve your tension. There are myriad strategies to resolve tension: sex, anger, fighting, eating, avoiding, numbing out with TV/drugs/ alcohol/computer games, excessive working, etc. Notice what you are moved to do to resolve your tension.

Step 3

Start to consider *not* resolving your tension. Take these actions when you are in tension:

- Acknowledge what you are thinking and feeling.
- Ask yourself: What would I love right now?
- Take action towards what you would love.
- Be gentle with yourself, this is just the beginning.

Identifying Your Underlying Assumptions

Revealing, knowing, recognising and neutralising your underlying relationship assumptions is the single most powerful thing you can do to create the relationship that you would love, whether you are in an existing relationship or want to create a new one. It's a process that requires your will and focus.

For the vast majority of people, the underlying assumption is hidden under layers of thoughts and feelings, veiled in turbulent thinking and emotional turmoil. The thoughts and emotions that mask the underlying assumption often give no clue to it. So how do you identify it?

First, let us recap the formation of assumptions. Imagine arriving here in life as divine creative spirit. You expect to be greeted by pure parenting, parenting that meets *all* your needs and acknowledges your nature. No matter how wonderful the parents, there are always occasions in early childhood where the needs of the child aren't met by one or both parents.

Baby wants feeding, mama is driving, or on the phone, or on the toilet. Baby doesn't get fed immediately. This creates tension: baby cries – why are my needs not being met? Baby makes up a reason for this pain: I'm unlovable, I'm insignificant, I can't have what I want, etc.

There's your underlying assumption right there. Every human being goes through this wounding process in early childhood to a greater or lesser degree.

Living with the assumption creates a tension of its own. You can imagine how much pain is created for someone who's walking around believing that they're unlovable or unwanted, or insignificant, or that no one can be trusted.

Our natural human response to that tension/pain is to try, by hook or by crook, to make it go away – to resolve it. This is usually done by behaving in ways that test whether the assumption is true or not. Am I really wanted, am I loveable, am I powerless? I'll test this person to see if they *really* love me, I'll attempt to prove my power to see if I'm *really* powerless, I'll test this situation to see if I can *really* trust this person.

This approach is doomed to failure. Why? Because any behaviour designed to resolve tension invests all the power of your consciousness in the assumption that is causing the pain in the first place. Your focus is on the assumption. You are doomed to create situations that prove your assumption.

Your actions will prove to you that the other person doesn't love you (you *are* unlovable), that you don't really have any power (you *are* powerless), that you really can't trust anyone, etc. Here's a real-life example:

Underlying Assumption
I'm going to be let down.

Relationship Problem (as defined by person)
Partner is in control of me – his drinking is in control of me.

Thoughts About the Problem
It's frightening, dark and desperate. It causes instability, turbulence and disappointment. It causes hurt and pain and might turn to violence and complete loss of control. It creates complete chaos everyday, lots of adrenalin and high stress levels. It's a horrible pattern.

Emotions Experienced
Desperation, exhaustion, anger, dissatisfaction, fear (of something really bad happening, not knowing what that might be), guilt (for children).

Relationship Reality
Partner continually violates my trust –

forgets to get children from school, almost burns down the house when drunk, is never where he's supposed to be, etc.

In the example above, the unconscious focus on the assumption "I'm going to be let down" systematically generates a reality where the partner acts in ways that prove the assumption beyond any doubt. In this case, the subject ended the relationship because she couldn't tolerate the volatile behaviours of her partner.

The more power of your consciousness you invest in the assumption, the more incidents and circumstances you create that prove the assumption. Eventually there's enough proof for the assumption to become hardwired – now it's a belief.

The Role of Thoughts and Emotions

Remember, all of this is taking place primarily unconsciously, not in the rational, self-aware part of your being.

In your normal state, you experience the thoughts and emotions that go with the assumption, not the actual assumption itself. For example, I have a major underlying assumption that I'm powerless. When the power of my consciousness is focused on that assumption, I generally experience rage.

The thoughts that go with it include: *"Why am I not being listened to? It's always like this, why does it have to be like this?"* etc.

The section 'Thoughts, Emotions and Assumptions" (Part 7 (iv), page 201) gives the actual thoughts and emotions that people have experienced when having problems in their relationships, and then shows the underlying assumptions in their unconscious that generate those thoughts and emotions.

You will notice that the thoughts and emotions do not necessarily logically point to the assumption. The assumptions were revealed using the Creator Alignment Process, created by William Whitecloud (Part 7 (iii), page 197).

Your thoughts and emotions do not reflect reality.

If you grasp the concept that your thoughts and emotions are generated by the assumptions, you will begin to realise that your thoughts and emotions are not telling you anything about reality.

They are, in fact, leading you down the garden path. Left to run their own course, those thoughts and emotions will eventually corner you into resolving them. The emotions will intensify and the thoughts will get louder and louder, until you can no longer stand the state that you are in.

Then you'll be picking fights, having tantrums, withdrawing, manipulating, blabbing to your friends about your crappy partner, leaving your partner and so on – whatever your method of tension resolution happens to be.

If you're single, you will resolve the tension of your thoughts and emotions about relationships by telling others that the dating scene is rubbish, that all the good men/women are taken and that you're not ready for a relationship, etc. You may also find that you are reasoning with yourself about why you are single.

Once you have resolved your terrible tension, the resulting outcome will prove the rightness of your underlying assumption, reinforce your behaviour and recreate the same tired old reality that you have been putting up with for your whole life.

Of course, thoughts and emotions make you human, enrich your experience of the world and are inevitable. The wonderful part is that, even though they do not inform you about reality, they are a brilliant indicator of your underlying assumptions.

> The more you know about the thoughts and emotions that accompany your assumptions, the more easily you can identify where you have invested the power of your consciousness.

For example, when I feel rage, I know I'm investing the power of my infinite consciousness in my assumption that I'm powerless.

When I'm thinking obsessively about how my partner is distracted and doesn't know what's going on, is withholding affection and isn't available, etc., I know that I'm investing power in my assumption that I'm unlovable.

I'm still experiencing the thoughts and emotions, but I am also observing them. Seeing them gives me the option to shift the power into something else. It gives me the opportunity to realise what game I'm playing and switch my focus to creating a reality that I would love instead.

I can step in as the lighthouse keeper and move the searchlight onto what I would love to create.

Understanding which assumptions your thoughts and emotions arise from is the groundwork that allows you to create the relationship you would absolutely love.

Noticing Your Body

Your physical body is a great indicator of what is going on in your consciousness. Take a moment to observe yourself next time you are with your partner, or a potential partner. Notice your posture. Are you open in your chest (revealing your heart), your arms, in your general position?

Or are you contracted inwards, (protecting your heart)? Are your arms and legs crossed? Do you feel as though you are physically opening towards your partner/potential partner or shrinking away?

Experiment with breathing into your heart and opening your chest area when you are with a partner, even if you are just making the dinner or having a mundane conversation. Notice any difference in your thoughts and emotions.

For some of us, the body is an easier indicator to use than thoughts or emotions. If you find yourself contracting inwards, protecting your heart, not making eye contact and generally turning away from your partner/potential partner, ask yourself what is going on for you.

Practical Steps Towards Transformation

Step 1

Make it your intention to uncover your underlying assumptions, to reveal them to yourself.

Commit to this.

Every time you are having a problem in your relationship, or with your lack of relationship, take yourself through this simple conflict exercise, it takes less than ten minutes.

It's important to be really honest with yourself.

The more truthful you can be, the faster you will reveal your assumptions to yourself.

Don't judge your answers, don't censor yourself – just out with it!

Ask yourself:

1. What's the problem? Be precise. For example, *"I think my partner is cheating on me," "I can't seem to create the intimacy I want," "Our sex life sucks," "I'm the one who does all the work in the relationship,"* or *"There's no one out there for me."*

2. What are you thinking about this problem? What thoughts go with it? Put all the thoughts down as quickly as you can.

3. What are you feeling about this problem? What emotions are you experiencing?

4. Are these thoughts and emotions familiar to you? Have you experienced them before?

5. What are you assuming about yourself? For example, *"I can't trust anyone," "I'm powerless," "I can't have what I want," "I don't know what I want,"* or *"I'm not good enough.".*

6. What are you assuming about your partner, if you have one? For example, *"He/she doesn't want me," "He/she doesn't love me," "He/she sucks,"* or *"He/she isn't what I want."*

7. What are you assuming about the world generally? For example, *"It's not safe,"* or *"It doesn't want me."* Refer to the list of assumptions on pages 38 and 39 for examples.

The more you do this, the better you will get at identifying your underlying assumptions. Every time you are experiencing the thoughts and emotions you identify in questions 2 and 3, you have energy invested in your underlying assumption.

When there is energy invested in your underlying assumption, you *will* create it in your reality. If you train the searchlight on pirates, pirates is what you'll get! You are a very powerful being.

Step 2

Once you have completed the exercise, do nothing about it. Just observe. Resist the urge to make yourself (or anyone else) wrong.

Think of it as a science experiment!

Shifting the Power

So, by now you are beginning to understand and identify your major underlying assumptions, as well as the thoughts and emotions that go with them. You are also starting to see patterns in the way that you create relationships.

If not, go back and reread the previous section on identifying underlying assumptions, especially the Practical Steps Towards Transformation (pages 58–60).

Now that you are aware of your assumptions, what are you going to do about them? The answer is: nothing. You're not going to do anything about them, you're just going to let them be there. Know them and let them be.

> Any attempt to address the underlying assumption will invest the power of your infinite consciousness squarely back in the assumption.

There are a number of modalities that advise working on, dealing with or healing your beliefs and assumptions – killing and attacking pirates.

Forget about it! It doesn't work. You will just end up right back where you started with your focus on your assumption and squadrons of pirates.

Never mind the pirates, they can be there. Without the searchlight trained on them, they will blunder about in the darkness and have no effect in your life whatsoever.

Temptation

The same is true of whatever thoughts and emotions accompany these assumptions. Do nothing about them. Let them be there.

It is perhaps easier to let the assumptions 'just be there' than the thoughts and emotions that accompany them. After all, assumptions are a concept, but thoughts and emotions actually grip you.

Circulating thoughts often seem as though they will drive you crazy (in truth they won't). Some emotions are very consuming, like anger, for example.

Furthermore, we live in a society where many thoughts and emotions are not 'good'. They are to be avoided, got rid of, worked on, shifted into a higher vibration, etc.

The temptation, therefore, is to try to get rid of a thought or feeling that you are not enjoying, to get away from it by attempting to distract yourself in some way, like pushing it away, and/or especially by affirmative polarising.

Let me explain what I mean by affirmative polarising. Say you have a thought spinning round your mind like this: *"My partner is so mean with money, he/she always expects me to pay for everything."* This thought might come with anger, resentment, bitterness and so on.

You would not be enjoying thinking these thoughts and feeling these emotions. You would experience tension that you wanted to resolve. So you might say to yourself, *"No no, truthfully my partner is generous and always treats me well."* You have swung from one pole (the mean one) to the other (the generous one).

Since thoughts and emotions don't reflect reality, whatever you happen to be making up about your partner probably isn't the truth, but polarising won't change anything for you.

Polarising holds you to your original negative thought. Your consciousness is no dummy, it knows that when you polarise, you are secretly trying to cover up the negative thought. So don't bother.

Let the thoughts and emotions be there. Do nothing about them. You will still experience them, but as the observer – the lighthouse keeper. You will begin saying to yourself, *"Oh look at me being angry,"* or *"Ha ha brain, that's an interesting train of thought."* You may even begin to recognise your underlying assumptions rearing their heads via your thoughts and emotions.

Eventually, you will experience the great freedom and joy of finding the thoughts funny!

Being Guided by Feelings

There are a few self-help modalities currently circulating that advise being guided by your feelings. The basic idea is that some feelings are 'high' (read 'good') vibration (such as joy, happiness and elation) and some are 'low' (read 'bad') vibration (anger, resentment, sadness, depression).

In a feelings-based model, the main aim of the game is to shift out of the 'low' vibration feelings and into the 'high' vibration feelings, by acknowledging those feelings. The theory is that by doing this you will attract 'high' vibration desires into your life.

It seems reasonable at first glance. However, as you already know, your feelings are not an indicator of reality, they inform you of your underlying assumptions.

Furthermore, as an infinite creative being, your human experience is coloured and enriched by many different experiences and feelings. As an infinite being, none of these are bad or good, high or low vibration. They just 'are'. Granted, some are more enjoyable to experience than others, but they have *nothing to do with your ability to create what you love.*

That's right. You can 'feel' totally crappy and *still* create the relationship you would love to be a part of. You can 'feel' absolutely wonderful, take no action towards what you would love and create nothing at all.

When I first met my partner, I 'felt' absolutely awful about the relationship. My underlying assumptions had all the power: I assumed I couldn't have what I wanted, that I was unworthy and unlovable. If I had been guided by the emotions that accompanied the assumptions, I would have immediately quit the relationship and missed out on one of the most fulfilling and delightful things in my life.

Your inherent nature as a human being is that of a creator. You are here to create, you can't help creating, you do it even if you don't want to!

It's possible that you may 'feel' a little overwhelmed at the prospect of being the creator of your experience. That's OK – it's a feeling, not a reflection of reality!

> The emotions you experience during the journey are part of the ride, neither good nor bad and they do not affect your ability to create what you love.

Notice your emotions and what they tell you about your underlying assumptions.

In Summary

Here are some key points to remember that will help you take the power out of your underlying assumptions:

- Know that whenever there is trouble in your relationship, your underlying assumption has the power.
- Know that when you are fighting with your partner, *your* underlying assumption has the power.
- Know that whenever you go to create, your underlying assumptions will rise up and attempt to keep you in your safe, comfortable patterns. They will have a try at getting the power.
- Know that the more you neutralise your underlying assumptions by recognising them and allowing them to be there, the less power they will have over time and the more you will create the relationship of your dreams.

- Know that your thoughts and emotions are not a guide to the state of your relationship (or lack of).

Once you have practised this for a while, you will gain the confidence of experience. You will find that you can recognise the signs of an assumption having the power (through your thoughts and emotions) and shift your focus to what you would love. You will discover that you can rapidly identify your underlying assumptions and learn to live with the tension they create.

Awareness of Your Addictions

> Your thought patterns and emotional states are addictive. These addictions keep you from receiving the relationship of your wildest dreams.

You may have seen *What the Bleep Do We Know*, 2004. It's a wonderful movie. There's a scene at a wedding where all the characters, lubed up by copious amounts of alcohol and good cheer, descend into their various emotional addictions, illustrated absolutely beautifully by deliciously awful animated characters. It's not a pretty sight.

In your intimate relationships you repeat certain strategies and behaviours. These behaviours lead to emotional states and thought patterns that you are utterly addicted to, despite the fact that they are generally very uncomfortable to experience.

Like everyone else, you will use your intimate relationship as a kind of needle for injecting your addictions and getting your hit.

You will 'set-up' certain scenarios which then trigger your addictive emotions and thoughts. Once you understand this, you will easily identify these addictions.

Which emotions that you would consider 'negative' do you mainly experience in your relationships? Answer immediately, without thinking. Write it down.

If you have habitually failed to create a lasting relationship, ask yourself which 'negative' emotion(s) you experience when you think about having a relationship.

You will have a thorough and tenacious addiction to these emotions, whether it be anger, resentment, hurt, despair, sadness, depression, fear etc. You have cultivated these addictions since childhood.

Sounds terrible doesn't it, but once you can see your addictions, they can be quite funny.

My personal favourite is feeling hurt. I unconsciously construct scenarios and conversations where my partner will say or do something which I find very hurtful. Then I feel terrible. I may cry. I used to ring my friends and howl to them. It's absolutely horrible to go through, but at the same time I am aware of a certain satisfaction at some level in my being. I'm getting my fix!

Nowadays, I usually recognise what I'm doing whilst I'm still in the set-up phase and pull out. If I'm unable to extract myself straight away, I recognise the addiction for what it is as soon as I begin to feel hurt. It then becomes very obvious to me how I set it up.

This addiction to feeling hurt isn't something I began recently. I have created very painful situations in my intimate relationships since day dot. I've been setting up this particular scenario for as long as I can remember.

Why? Because it confirms for me over and over and over again that I'm unlovable and I can't have what I want. That's one of my underlying assumption: *I'm unlovable (and always will be) and I can't have what I want.*

The most insidious thing about these addictions is that no matter how awful you feel when you find yourself in yet another scenario that proves your underlying assumption, at some level you are actually enjoying the emotion that you're experiencing.

In some part of my being, I sadistically enjoy feeling tragically hurt, but not consciously. What is taking place is this: whilst I am in a relationship receiving love, my experience is in direct conflict with my underlying assumption that I'm unlovable. This creates extreme tension. Once I have created a situation where I feel hurt, that tension is relieved.

Consciously it's very painful to experience the emotion, but truthfully at some other level, I love it because I am no longer in conflict with my assumption! How weird is that? In addition, there are pathways in the brain that are associated with repeated behaviour patterns. The rush of relief from tension and the experience of feeling hurt come with a release of chemicals into the brain. My body is joining in! This constitutes an addiction.

If I'm really caught up, I'll play the hurtful comment over and over again in my mind (this is where a photographic memory comes is really useful) until I'm in such a state that it seems like there's no longer any point in living. It's addictive and repetitive.

Emotional Freedom

Noticing

The first way to begin to free yourself from addictive emotions is to recognise them. The more familiar you can become with your addictions and how they play out, the less power they will have.

How do you do this? NOTICE. Be aware of yourself in your relationships. When things go wrong and you are gripped by powerful emotions – anger, despair, frustration – ask yourself, *"What's actually happening here? Is this something that has happened before? What emotion am I experiencing?"*

You will begin to see a pattern emerging. Have patience. If you really commit to knowing yourself, the beautiful pageant of your complex human nature will unveil itself to you like a deep, clear pool filling from many tributaries.

The Set-up

Secondly, once you are familiar with your addiction, begin to notice how you set it up. You will be astonished by the repetition of events. You will start to hear yourself saying the things that lead to scenarios that fuel your addictions and you'll be amazed.

As an imperfect (but wonderful) human being, I still sometimes create my partner saying hurtful things. They still hurt. But now I also laugh about it and congratulate myself on my amazing creative abilities.

Allow

Do not try to stop yourself from indulging in your addictive states. Resistance will only lead to more of the same. If you have created a relationship scenario where you are experiencing addictive emotions and thoughts, just allow them to be there.

Be aware at the same time, that what you are experiencing is not reality, it's a function of your addictions and doesn't mean anything.

Incompleteness

One way or other, usually unconsciously, we all believe we are incomplete, not whole. This is implicit in your underlying assumptions.

If the power of your consciousness is in your underlying assumptions, you are also assuming that you are not complete – that you are not a whole person and that there's something 'out there' that will make you a whole person. *Only then* can you have the relationship that you truly desire.

Unluckily for us, once we're grown up and can no longer test our assumptions on our parents, we tend to push for our partners to validate these assumptions. We're looking for a relationship to make us feel complete, to mask and resolve the unpleasant thoughts and emotions that accompany the underlying assumptions. What generally ends up happening is that your relationship just provides more proof of your incompleteness.

If you enter into and function within your relationship from this incompleteness, you will prove your incompleteness through the relationship. Your partner will provide all the evidence you could ever require and you will be at the very least, unhappy.

That's why your intimate relationship is really the last bastion for all your crap to play out. Even people who are committed to taking total responsibility for what takes place in their relationship are still tempted to complain about their partner, as though something is happening *to* him/her. It's part of the mass collusion of our society.

Your relationship is the final frontier, the perfect playground to achieve self-mastery. If you can create what you would love in your relationship, the rest of the world is easy, nothing will stop you *and* you will have the beautiful, satisfying connection with another human being that you dream of.

> Here's the beastly news:
> You are a complete being now.
> Your infinite creative being is always present.

Just take the time to digest that. *You are a complete being now.* Imagine that.

What if you are already complete? What if there's nothing you need to *do* about yourself, add to yourself, fix, heal or improve? What if you can just *have* the relationship of your wildest dreams?

Stew on that for a while, it's an absolute life changer.

Stop whining to your friends about all the things that you don't like in your relationship or your partner. Use your imagination. Tell people about what you'd love to create, what would truly make your heart sing. Assume that you are whole and complete. You're creating just for the pure, unadulterated joy of it.

If everything has gone wrong and you absolutely must blab about it to someone, do the conflict process on pages 59–60 and then share your answers with someone. Keep it about you. Use it as an opportunity to understand yourself better. Then move on, tell that person what you would love, even if your addictions are attempting to keep you in a miserable state. You have a choice.

In Summary

- To neutralise your underlying assumptions, allow them to be there with any accompanying thoughts and emotions. Acknowledge what's going on and *do nothing about it.*
- Commit to recognising your addictive emotions and thought patterns.
- Know that you are a complete being right now.

PART 3

Common Relationship Dynamics Dynamited

Common Relationship Dynamics Dynamited

This chapter has all the juicy stuff in it (except for lovemaking, which is covered later). So far we have focused on you, what you have created in the past and how you have created it.

This part of the book deals with the dynamics that take place within relationships that are often dramatised, exaggerated, labelled as dysfunctional and given as reasons for ending a relationship. These dynamics can seem very powerful because they are highly colluded upon aspects of 'how it is' in relationships.

In order to create the relationship of your wildest dreams, it's important to let go of 'how it is' and give yourself the space to receive your own wisdom.

Collusion

We'll address collusion first, because even though it takes place outside your relationship, colluding is one of the first things many of us do when we encounter trouble with a partner. In the sections that follow, you will recognise many topics that are widely colluded on amongst friends and in the media.

One of the fastest, easiest and deadliest ways to put the kibosh on what you would love to create, is to collude. The Oxford Dictionary definition of collude is *"come to an understanding or conspire together"*. In other words, it is agreeing with others about 'how it is'.

Typically this involves telling others what your partner is like (and what men/women are like) and then seeking validation and/or approval of this opinion. You are actually conspiring with whomever you are talking to about the way you believe your situation/the world/other people to be.

For example:

"Tony is always coming home late, he just doesn't realise that I need him home to help with the kids."

Or,

Person 1: *"I just feel like I can't trust him. You know how that is."*
Person 2: *"Ooh yes, I hate that."*

Or even,

Person 1: *"Women are so emotionally needy."*
Person 2: *"You're so right, mate."*

Colluding is when you start telling others (and especially yourself) how things are with your partner, what your partner is like, how the relationship is – particularly when it's something that you don't like. In other words, you focus on what is outside of you (ie. your partner and their behaviour, the relationship, other people etc).

You imagine you are sharing your feelings with your friend/parent/counsellor, but what you are actually doing is training your searchlight on what you don't want, on your underlying assumptions. As you do this, the power is leaching out of what you would truly love to create with your partner. You are creating your reality as you speak and it's not the one you truly want.

Listen to Yourself

Ultimately, your life will be transformed when you quit colluding altogether, but before you stop colluding, start listening to what you say to others about your partner or about creating a relationship.

Listen for your underlying assumptions. Let yourself collude, but hear your words with the intention of identifying your underlying assumptions. If the person you are talking to joins in with what you are saying, agrees with you, or encourages you in your collusion, just take no notice. They are only doing what you are unconsciously willing them to do. It means nothing.

This may seem like a wild and unlikely claim, but if you stopped all colluding about your relationship today – that means not one word to a single soul about how you believe your partner is, or what you think your relationship is like – you would be astonished by the change in the energy between you and your partner and the space that is generated to create something different.

If you are not in a relationship, your collusion will be around the stories you tell yourself and others about why you are not in a relationship. Maybe you make jokes about not finding the right person. Perhaps you put yourself down, even if you are being humorous. If you listen to these stories, your underlying assumptions will jump right out at you.

Once you have identified your underlying assumptions, stop colluding.

For more assistance with identifying underlying assumptions see 'Identifying Your Underlying Assumptions', page 51.

Fighting

When you fight or have heated arguments with your partner, it is always your attempt to resolve the tension and pain created by your underlying assumptions.

For example, someone with an underlying assumption of powerlessness will continually create a reality where it appears as though their partner is trying to control them or has the power in the relationship – their thoughts and feelings are constantly telling them this is the case.

This creates psychological pain and tension that is begging to be resolved. It happens to me – I start thinking that my partner is trying to control me or manipulate my behaviour. I begin to feel irritated and on edge.

Sooner or later the 'powerless' person will attempt to either wrestle the power off their partner, or will instigate passive aggressive tactics to assert their own power. Before you know it, there's conflict under way.

Returning to the model of *It's All You*, what you are actually doing when you are fighting is getting into conflict with yourself. You are creating the whole fight and driving it forwards with the tension of your underlying assumptions. You are fighting yourself.

In my own case, once I'm feeling edgy, I want to make snide comments, I become watchful and ready to bite back. If I act in favour of those thoughts and emotions, the situation will worsen and my tension will increase.

If I continue to act in favour of those thoughts and emotions, I will eventually start a fight (during which my partner will inevitably say something terribly hurtful!). This usually ends up proving one or more of my underlying assumptions.

I am laughing as I write this because it's actually funny that I can create like this. My limited self is very reliable!

The beautiful thing about conflict is that if you pay attention while it's happening, you will receive the most amazing insights into your assumptions and behaviours.

Practical Conflict

It takes time and practice to master, but try this.

Next time you are in conflict with your partner, pay attention to what you are saying and to the behaviours you are exhibiting. Ask yourself: *"Which of my major underlying assumptions do these words and actions belong with? What triggered my response?"*

Write your answers down.

If you are not currently in a relationship, there will (no doubt) be occasions where you are in conflict with others: work colleagues, family members and so on.

Even if you are not openly fighting and the conflict is mainly going on in your head, ask the question: Which of my major underlying assumptions do these thoughts belong with? What triggered this?

It Means Nothing

It doesn't seem possible, but contrary to commonly held belief, the fights you have mean *nothing*. You can totally disregard everything that was said by you or your partner. It means absolutely nothing. It's complete nonsense driven by the tension of underlying assumptions and can be written off as tension resolution.

> A fight is a way to resolve your tension.
> Nothing more.

That's the key, it really does mean nothing – about you, about your partner, about the relationship, about your ability to create what you would love. *Nothing*, get it, nothing!

Despite this, people love to attribute meaning to fighting. Here are some common conclusions:

- I/my partner needs to apologise.
- We need to talk it over (endlessly until one person concedes they behaved badly).
- My partner doesn't love me.
- Our relationship is stuffed/over/headed for the rocks.
- This always happens to me.
- I am a bad person/my partner is a bad person.
- This shouldn't happen in a loving relationship.

You do not need to apologise and nor does your partner. People make the the most repulsive and outrageous verbal attacks on their partners during conflict, but still it means nothing.

Even if, during a big spat, he/she your partner expressly said,

"I don't love you. You are my worst nightmare. I hate all of your family and am never going there for Christmas again, plus you are too fat for me. I wish I had never left my husband for you ... blah blah," do not take him/her at their word.

I know this sounds a bit mad, but the only reason for you to listen to abusive and depressing statements during a fight is to hear your assumptions.

Why? Because *It's All You.* The model of this whole book. If your partner has said ghastly things to you, it's purely driven by your underlying assumptions, that's all.

The big bonus is, that if you listen to what your partner is saying in a fight, you will hear the subtext of your underlying assumptions.

I remember years ago when I was first married, fighting with my ex-husband. At the peak of the yelling, he shouted that it was no wonder my Dad left the family when I was a child and that it would definitely have been my fault.

When I look back on it, it seems very funny, but at

the time I was completely crushed. Not only that, I actually considered that he might be telling the truth (I was seven when my Dad left my mother for another woman).

Clearly it's absurd. But back then I was completely shocked and depressed for days. If it happened now, I would know that what I was hearing was the result of my focus being on my underlying assumption that I'm unlovable. The comment would still hurt, but now I can see it for what it is and ignore it – it means nothing.

> Conflict shows you what you are focused on.

The same applies to anything you might have said to your partner. It doesn't matter. It was driven by your underlying assumptions and is meaningless. There's no need to agonise over what was said. Acknowledge to yourself that the fight is what happens when your assumptions have the power.

Know Thyself

It's boring, I know, that I keep harping on about this, but the more you know and understand what limits you (your underlying assumptions), the more you will free yourself to create a relationship you will truly love.

When you are fighting, try to observe yourself. Say to yourself, *"Look at me throwing a tantrum,"* or (my favourite), *"Here's me behaving badly,"* or something similar. If you acknowledge yourself in this way *during* the fight, often all of the fight will drain out of you.

Over time, you will find that you just can't be bothered continuing the argument or that you are still arguing but without caring about the outcome – half juiced up instead of fully raging! Or you may suddenly see the funny side and start laughing.

Conventional wisdom will tell you that if you've had a fight with your partner, you need to 'work it out', have counselling, apologise, try to find common ground, take responsibility for your part in it and the same for your partner etc. This is hogwash.

You were fighting with yourself, no further action is required with your partner. This can be a tough one to swallow as you may be used to an illusion of 'making it up' after a fight.

Furthermore, fighting is not *bad*, no matter what revolting things you may have said to each other or how many dinners you flung. Fighting isn't a bad or wrong thing to do, it was just you resolving your tension, no big deal.

So What Do I Do Then?

Resist the urge to make yourself or your partner wrong.

After an argument/fight, do not talk it over – that's just more of the same attempt to resolve tension. The fight means zip, nada, nix, nothing. Forget it. It just means you had a fight. So what, humans do it, it's inevitable. Accept that it's no big deal.

If your partner's words come back and haunt you, learn to dismiss them as nonsense created by you having the power of your consciousness squarely parked in your underlying assumptions.

If you keep hearing some mean comment of theirs cycling round in your head, understand that what you are doing is trying to wallow in an emotional state that you are addicted to. Ask yourself: *"Which of my underlying assumptions could this relate to?"* Acknowledge it.

Hopefully you were paying attention during the conflict and learned something about yourself. Once a fight is over, note to yourself that this was you resolving your tension and throwing a tantrum. Notice how you behaved, what you said and did and what unfolded as a result.

Important: I am not suggesting that you pretend the fight didn't happen. It did happen. Your job is to tell the truth about it – you created it, however unwittingly. *It's All You,* remember. Acknowledge what took place and which assumptions had the power, and move on.

The Right Stuff

It takes courage and substance to go beyond your own ideas about what has taken place in a fight, and also beyond all the conventional wisdom that says that fighting is wrong and bad, and dictates what *should* happen afterwards (apologies and counselling).

In the beginning, when you start to approach things differently, you may find that the conventional 'shoulds' are even louder than usual, that your desire to resolve tension is even stronger than usual.

This is normal and is your limited self making a stand – the underlying assumptions in your consciousness are freaking out because they don't have the power any more. Initially, when you take the searchlight away from the monkey, the monkey will have a go at taking it back. He/she may get aggressive and try to bite!

Mythologically speaking, you are facing a dragon. The dragon's job is to hold you in your old patterns and protect your heart at all costs. This can be quite frightening and you may feel as though you, others or the situation are out of control.

Do not be deterred. If you have journeyed this far into the book, you can assure yourself that you have the required substance to pacify the dragon and create what you love.

Know that each time you use a fight to take the opportunity to know yourself more and disregard your desire to resolve tension, you are cultivating substance, backbone, character – whatever you want to call it. You are developing 'the right stuff'!

Developing an ability to engage your backbone and not resolve your tension will serve you tremendously in conflict situations – internal or external.

Violence in Relationships

If you or your partner use more than words during a conflict, there will inevitably be consequences. Violence is born of rage. Rage is the emotion that arises from an assumption of powerlessness. If you allow your rage to drive you to physical violence against people or objects, you have invested a huge portion of your powerful creative consciousness in your underlying assumption – what a waste of your creative power.

Furthermore, this will inevitably produce a reality that is most unenjoyable, as well as consequences that only prove your powerlessness – such as encounters with authority figures (such as police and the legal system). There's nothing like being incarcerated in a huge, faceless authoritarian system to reinforce a powerless belief.

That potent, overwhelming sense of rage can be dealt with in other ways.

- Start by acknowledging its source – a deeply held belief/assumption that you are powerless.
- Acknowledge possible consequences of acting on the assumption.
- Release pent up energy from your body in another way. For example, go outside and yell very loudly, run, swim, whatever works for you.
- Catch yourself early on. Recognise the signs of powerless rage building and nip it in the bud. Dismiss your assumption – it isn't real.
- Get some help that works for you. There are numerous community and government organisations that assist in domestic violence situations.
- Refocus on what you would love (see Part 4, page 97).
- Spend time investing your energy in activities that truly matter to you. Give yourself what you love.

And the Victims of Violence

The key word here is victim. Alternative meanings: sufferer, casualty, injured party, martyr – in other words, one to whom things are done. Powerless.

If you think of yourself as a victim, you are disempowering yourself. You may have created this reality unconsciously, but you always have the creative power to change it.

If we bring it back to the original premise – *It's All You* – at some level you are creating the violence of which you are a victim. This can be a fearful premise to face, but it also puts the creation of your reality back in your hands.

You may also be addicted to the drama and pain of being violated. Isolating your underlying assumption(s) and putting the power of your consciousness in what you would love will radically change your situation.

Obviously, if your current reality includes a violent partner, it's in the interests of your heart to remove yourself from that person whilst you begin to understand yourself and the way that you create relationships. Government and community agencies can assist you with this step.

Pain

Which brings us to pain. It is a common collusion in our culture that physical pain is much harder to endure and somehow more painful than other kinds of pain (mental, emotional, etc.).

The pain generated by physical abuse is no more or less painful than that produced by verbal abuse – both of these being perceived as visited upon you.

Pain created from within by thoughts and emotions associated with underlying assumptions can be just as painful as pain in your physical body (so much so that it drives people to suicide).

Pain is pain – no matter what the perceived cause – it hurts and can be very addictive. All pain hurts, but just like conflict, it doesn't mean anything about you, your partner, your ability to create or about the world. It's just pain and it hurts, that's all.

We are all powerful creative beings. The current reality that you have created where you appear to be a victim is not set in stone. You can change it by recognising where the power of your consciousness is invested and shifting your focus to what you would love.

You can train your searchlight on what you want to create. You are the lighthouse keeper.

This may or may not mean abandoning your existing relationship. Extraordinary things happen when you take the power out of your underlying assumptions and put it into what you would truly love – including quite inexplicable and radical changes in the people around you.

Boring Old Blame

Yawn. Blame is for victims, not powerful creative beings. Most of us like to blame others for what takes place in life. It feels good to make the bits of life we don't like someone else's fault.

However, once you begin to dabble in the premise *It's All You*, it can be very tempting to blame yourself for your creations.

> Self-blame is futile and a total waste of your energy. It puts the searchlight squarely back on your underlying assumptions.

Joseph Campbell, inspiring human, professor of mythology and author of *Pathways to Bliss* (and many other wonderful books) said, *"Our job is not to blame or explain, our job is to handle the life that arises."*

Forget about blame and about trying to work out why events have taken place. Keep your focus on what you would love.

If you've created a crappy reality attempting to resolve the tension of your underlying assumptions, recognise it, see what you can learn from it and then refocus and forget about it. It means nothing about you, the world or what you are able to create.

I'll give you a personal example. Some time after my partner and I had been trying for another baby, I got pregnant (not my first). At almost six weeks pregnant, I was rushed to hospital and whisked into emergency surgery for an ectopic pregnancy (where the embryo is lodged in the fallopian tube and begins to grow there).

My left tube had ruptured and I was bleeding into my pelvis. Without surgery I would have died. The pregnancy was terminated and the embryo sent off to a pathology lab somewhere. I was shocked and sad. It took a while to recover physically; I had infected wounds, stitches in existing scar tissue and other troublesome symptoms.

The whole scenario caused me a lot of pain – physical and emotional. It took about six weeks to recover from the basic experience of surgery, healing and grieving.

That could have been an end to it and I could have gone back to creating what I love. However, I made myself absolutely miserable for several months afterwards trying to work out *how* it happened.

The main culprit in my mind was me – I created that, why did I create that, how did I create that, how could I avoid something similar in the future?

In other words, I blamed myself. I even spent a short while trying to blame my partner – perhaps he had the power in an underlying assumption that meant that the pregnancy went wrong!

Did I get anywhere with this? Hell no! All that wrangling and blaming just held me in my underlying assumptions: I'm powerless and I can't have what I want. The more examination I did, the worse my existence became – depression, frustration and misery.

I invested all the considerable power of my consciousness in my assumptions. It was a lonely, dismal reality that stretched out interminably to the point where I couldn't stand to be around newborn babies at all, or even see them in the street. I wanted to spend my time in my wardrobe where I wouldn't see anything that might upset me!

The minute I let it all go and stopped trying to find somewhere to park the blame for the loss of the baby, life improved. Once I had refocused and invested my energy in what I love, life opened up before me again, magical and full of potential.

Furthermore, I made the whole thing mean nothing. It only meant that I lost a pregnancy, not anything about me, my partner or my ability to create.

You want to create bliss and magic for yourself? Leave blame behind, right here on this page – the only place where it belongs.

In Summary

- Listen for your underlying assumptions when you collude. Aim to stop colluding.
- Conflict isn't bad. It's a great opportunity to learn more about yourself and it means nothing.
- Notice your urge to resolve tension by fighting. Cultivate the right stuff – courage and substance.

- Know that if you do fight, you are really only fighting yourself.
- Violence in relationships is driven by an underlying assumption of powerlessness in both the violent party and the 'victim'.
- Pain hurts but, like fighting, it doesn't mean anything.
- Blaming yourself for relationship stuff-ups will only train your searchlight back on your underlying assumptions. So don't bother.

"Life is a great big canvas, and you should throw all the paint you can on it."

Danny Kaye

PART 4

Creating the Relationship of Your Dreams

Creating the Relationship of Your Dreams

So, we're about half way through this incredible journey. It's a great time to remind you that you don't need to *believe* what I'm saying to create the relationship of your wildest dreams.

You may think that I'm completely batty, that's OK. The important question is, are you experimenting with the model *It's All You*?

If you are, you will be noticing changes in yourself and, if you have one, your partner. If you're not using the model, start now – have a go, you've got nothing to lose and you don't need to believe it for it to work.

What Would You Love?

OK, so you've taken the power of your infinite creative consciousness out of your underlying assumptions by becoming aware of them, recognising the thoughts and emotions that go with them and beginning to see patterns in your creating.

Now what? Where are you going to put that power?

> The question now is
> what would you love to create?

If you put your thoughts, feelings and assumptions to one side, *what relationship would you love to create?* Whether you have an existing relationship or not, you *must* ask yourself this question.

You need your imagination for this. There is no right answer, it's what *you* would love to create, not what your mother thinks would be great for you, not what you think you should have or what your friend has, not what someone else says would be great for you, not what you need to complete you. Purely and simply what *you* would love, whatever that is.

When I started asking myself this question, I'd spent so many years focused on all the things I hated about my relationship that it was actually difficult to come up with what I *did* want.

So I started small, I was just getting used to the idea that I could actually create what I wanted. I asked myself what I would love to create in a relationship and the answer was that I would love a man that would dance with me. That was the beginning.

Start somewhere, it doesn't have to be grand. Look into your own heart, what is it that you would truly love? Write it down right now.

Shifting Your Focus

So far we've primarily dealt with your limited self and its preoccupations: trying to be complete, addictions, underlying assumptions etc. That's all well and good and absolutely critical to explore if you want to create a truly magical relationship. However, at this point we're going to shift the focus.

You are now going to step in as the lighthouse keeper, take hold of the searchlight and train it on what you would love, what you would *truly* love.

There is a strange and insidious phenomenon that takes place when people get acquainted with their patterns and assumptions and that is, that they then become identified with those patterns and assumptions.

So instead of complaining or colluding or telling tales about their dismal, unsatisfactory, useless partner or how hard it is to find a partner, a person will begin complaining, colluding and telling tales about their own shortcomings.

So you hear someone saying, *"Well, you know, I do have this tendency to be let down by the masculine,"* or *"Well I have this powerless thing going and it means blah blah blah happens."* To be blunt, who cares? Boring, boring, boring!

What's required here is a complete shift in how you think about yourself and others, not simply shifting the whining and colluding from others to yourself.

Know your assumptions and the thoughts, emotions and behaviours that go with them, and then shift your focus. Don't whine to people about them, don't wear them like a badge, just know them.

We've already done a fair amount of focus shifting. You've shifted the focus off your partner and others 'out there' and onto yourself, taken responsibility for your creating. That's an awesome step.

Now, you're going to shift the focus onto what you would love to create. You are going to dream about what you would love, write about what you would love, talk about it to anyone who'll listen and take it into your being as though it were already real. You are going to do this whether you are already in a relationship or are about to create one.

Of course, before you can do that, you need to know *what* you would truly love. Luckily this book comes with a couple of methods for finding that out without the know-it-all interference of your rational mind (via your thoughts and emotions).

Discovering What You Would Truly Love

It's important to distinguish between the relationship you would *truly* love to create from your infinite creative being, and the relationship you *think* you would love from your rather limited mind.

We're going to go deeper now into what you would truly love, connect with your infinite creative being and find out what the relationship you would love actually looks and feels like.

There are a couple of useful tools for doing this, both of them are based in an amazing and extraordinary power that we all have – intuition.

Intuition is a perfectly ordinary (yet magical) human skill that can be effectively utilised by anyone, including you. Like most things, it improves with practice. Plus, it's fun!!!

Perhaps you've read this book to this point and said to yourself, *"OK, well this lady has a few interesting points, she might be a bit mad, but I'll keep going with it and see what happens."* Lovely, I'm very happy that you're still with me.

What I am about to present to you is an absolutely invaluable tool that you can use in any area of your life.

> Using your intuition will revolutionise the way
> that you see and experience your reality.

Learning to use your intuition is just as important as experimenting with the model of this book – *It's All You*.

Allow any doubts you might have about your intuitive ability to be present and embrace the next part of the book. Everyone can do this and do it well with practice.

You will be amazed!

Meet Your Soul Partner Meditation

It's important that you reveal to yourself what you would truly love in a relationship. It is time to lift the veil of your thoughts and emotions and powerfully reveal the qualities and essence of the relationship of your wildest dreams, the one that you would truly love to live. We will use a guided meditation for this.

The meditation is an intuitive process designed to connect you to your heart and allow you to receive your truth without the filters of your underlying assumptions. It will put your searchlight squarely on the relationship of your dreams.

The simplest and most effective way to use the

meditation is to download the audio included with this book, which you will find at:

http://www.pollyannadarling.com/rraudio.html

Alternatively, find some time when you won't be disturbed and ask a friend to read the meditation to you (see Part 7 (ii), page 194). The meditation will not be as effective if you simply read through it yourself. Take action in favour of what you would love and allow yourself to be guided, so that all you have to do is receive.

Be open to receiving the wisdom of your heart and listen to the meditation with a pen and paper standing by to capture your impressions.

————————————

Welcome back! So, you will have captured some of the qualities and essence of the relationship you would love to create and of your soul partner. You may have met a person you actually know, a mythic being or just an energy – it doesn't matter. Try not to be too literal with what you have received.

If Nelson Mandela was waiting for you, it does not literally mean that Nelson Mandela is your soul partner! In a scenario like that, you would interpret Nelson as a symbol – what does he mean to you? What are the qualities that you believe he possesses that appeal to you, that you resonate with?

Focus on the vibration and quality of your soul partner and what you would love. Stay connected to *that* while we journey deeper into the relationship of your dreams.

Now, we'll get into the juicy stuff and start using your intuition in a structured way to find out more about the relationship you would love.

Be aware that what you are learning can be applied to anything that you would love to create, in any area of your life.

Using Your Intuition to Discover Your Truth

What is Intuition?

The dictionary definition of intuition is *"immediate apprehension by the mind without reasoning."* That means: what you immediately receive or understand before your busy mind begins adding beliefs, thoughts, feelings and what it already knows, to the information you are receiving.

Because you are an infinitely creative being, you are connected to all things through all time and space, despite anything you may think. As an infinite being, you have access to extraordinary gifts, abilities and information. One of them is intuition – an ability that enables you to gather information on any topic you can come up with, without using your thinking brain.

Everyone has intuitive ability, including you! Who can say where intuition actually comes from. Personally, I imagine a layer of information somewhere out there in the ether, that I tap into when I am choosing to use my intuition – an intuitive realm.

Why Use Intuition?

You have, like every other human, accumulated a collection of underlying assumptions, thoughts and emotions that limit your potential. When you make decisions based on those assumptions, thoughts and emotions, you are limiting what's possible in your life, your relationships, your mind and your consciousness.

When you act in favour of those limiting assumptions, thoughts and emotions, you are acting in favour of a limited reality, often a reality that is not as you would love it to be.

Your intuitive voice is the voice of your heart – your infinitely creative being.

The intuitive voice is often quieter than the constant, chattery noise of assumptions, thoughts and emotions. You will have experienced those times where a very little voice is quietly suggesting that you take a certain path of action, and your mind is loudly insisting that you take a different path. Some refer to this as 'gut feeling'.

This quieter voice is your intuitive voice – the voice of your divinely creative, infinite self.

It is also the voice of innocence, the part of you that has no preconceived ideas about 'how it is', 'how he/she is', 'how I am'. The part of you that can see all things as they truly are, that takes each moment as it comes, without bringing the past or the future into the equation.

When you listen to and act on your intuitive voice, you are acting in favour of your highest potential, the limitless possibility of the extraordinary being that you are. You are outside your thoughts, emotions and assumptions, free to create and experience the true magic of life.

Your intuitive capacity is the most powerful tool you can use to create the relationship you would love. The limited self is generally a very unreliable source of information about what you truly love. When you enquire into what you would love, your mind may give you false guidance, coming up with strategies to keep you safe, powerful, aloof, estranged, enraged, etc.

Your rational mind is excellent for managing projects, doing mathematics, spelling, using language and so on, but no use at all for establishing what truly matters to you. It's too clouded by your thoughts, emotions and assumptions.

Your intuition is always reliable, sometimes illogical and using it has extraordinary results.

For example, I had been squabbling with my partner and felt morose and depressed. I was sitting on the beach plagued by thoughts about how annoying, droopy and overbearing he was. I remembered (before I had completely slumped) that I could use my intuition to discover what was going on for me, as well as what I would love.

So I followed the procedure described in the next section to find out what I would love, which was to receive my partner from his divinely creative, beautiful self.

Immediately afterwards, my emotions (which had been pretty overwhelming) calmed down. I focused my attention on seeing my partner in his infinite, creative self and relaxed. When he came home later that day, he had bought me flowers and we spent a delicious evening together.

Imagine your intuitive capacity as a muscle: the more you flex it, the stronger it gets. The more practice you have in using your intuitive ability, the stronger it becomes and the easier it is to hear your intuitive voice.

The Relationship of Your Dreams

Let's use your intuitive muscle to tune into the relationship of your dreams. 'Tuning in' is when you access the intuitive realm I referred to earlier. Once you have access, you will receive information that is outside your thoughts, emotions, assumptions and often your prior knowledge.

The intuitive realm is accessed by using circles. Circles were *temenos* to the Greeks – a boundary between the sacred and the divine and have been used for centuries by many cultures to create a space for sacred work.

In the beginning, find a time when you won't be disturbed. As your intuitive voice becomes louder through use, you will be able to access the intuitive realm wherever you are, no matter what is going on around you.

Audio Guidance

If you would prefer to be guided through this process, I have created an audio file for you. You can download it at:

> http://www.pollyannadarling.com/rraudio.html.

It's the same process, but guided by me. You will need to have a paper and pen handy to write down what you receive.

Alternatively, you can follow the instructions

below. Read all the way through the instructions before you begin, so that you don't have to keep referring to them while you are tuning in.

By the way, if you are feeling a bit daunted by all this, just let that be there. With more practice and experience, you will be astonished by the ways in which using your intuition enriches your life.

Tips for Using Your Intuition

For the most effective use of your intuitive powers, take the following steps:

- Always choose to serve your heart before you begin.
- Drop into a state of innocence, let go of any need to know what you're going to get.
- Interpret your symbol (don't describe it). Run with what's obvious about your symbol and keep to what's obvious.
- Don't think about or analyse what you have received.
- Don't judge what you receive – your emotional responses to it are irrelevant.
- Don't worry about whether you are right or about getting more logical information.

We will begin with the vision of the relationship of your dreams. This is what you would love to create, what makes your heart sing, what's possible for an infinitely creative being.

Vision

First, sit comfortably and take a few deep breaths, relaxing into your body as you exhale.

Now define a circle around you as your vision of the relationship of your dreams. Choose to serve your heart and to be in a state of innocence (a great way to do this is to imagine a photograph of yourself as a young child and then imaginatively step into that child).

Let go of any ideas and expectations you may have about the vision. Imagine a big, blank whiteboard right in front of you – make sure it's completely white. If there are any thoughts or emotions sneaking in, keep imagining the vast, blank whiteboard.

Now, imagine the circle of the relationship of your dreams vibrating with possibility, humming with potential.

Sit in that vibration until you feel yourself vibrating with the possibility. Now summon a symbol that will inform you about the vision of the relationship of your dreams. You can just say to yourself, *"Give me a symbol that will inform me about the vision of the relationship of my dreams."*

Your symbol can be anything, and I mean *absolutely* anything. Accept the first thing that comes to you, whether it's a frog, a spaceship, six red balls or a blank white line. You have received this symbol from the intuitive realm. Whatever you get is whatever you get.

Now look at the symbol in your mind's eye and assume that it is informing you of your vision of the relationship of your dreams. Now interpret that symbol.

Note: there are many different 'standard' interpretations for symbols (e.g. a snake can symbolise sexuality, or a dove – peace). What you are going to do is interpret whatever stands out to *you* about the symbol, regardless of its commonly held meaning.

It is very important to interpret your symbol. Don't describe it, that will limit you only to the characteristics of the symbol. When you interpret, you will go beyond the symbol, further information will come and you will go deeper and deeper into discovering your truth.

Interpret by talking or writing about what is obvious about the symbol (what jumps out at you about it) – interpret, don't describe. Keep talking/writing about what's obvious, make it up and ask yourself, *"What else is obvious?"*

Here's an example of a symbol interpretation on a relationship that someone would love. The symbol received was the Celtic Claddagh ring (one of the most famous Celtic ring designs: it has two hands holding a heart with a crown on top). This is an interesting symbol, because it has a known meaning, but I have interpreted what jumped out about it to *me*.

It's all about the heart and having the heart at the centre, almost as though the relationship itself has a heart and both people are supporting this heart. They are joined by the strength of the heart, it holds them together and is bright and strong. The strength of the relationship is in their hands. The heart is king.

That's just a very quick interpretation to give you the general idea.

Keep talking or writing. The more you talk/write, the more information will come to you. Don't worry if it doesn't make sense or seems impossible, just keep making it up.

Yes, you read that correctly, just make it up, use your boundless imagination to interpret your symbol. Give yourself the freedom to make it up based on what's obvious about your symbol.

Capture the qualities of the vision of the relationship of your dreams, the vibration, any feelings or images that go with it. The more you talk and write, the more information you will get. Allow your imagination to soar.

You may find that you do not have an emotional

connection to the vision. You may even have an adverse reaction to your vision (your mind might jump in and say, *"Pah, you can't have that!"*). Don't worry about it. Happily, your emotional response to the vision has nothing to do with whether you will love it or not! Remember, your thoughts and emotions are no reflection of reality, they are driven by your underlying assumptions.

Current Reality

Wipe away the previous circle now (I'm sure you have captured what you received). Imagine that vision circle disappearing.

Now define another circle around you as your current reality. This is where you are currently in relation to creating the relationship of your dreams.

It doesn't matter whether you are in a relationship or not, you can still receive a current reality. You will either get the current status of your relationship or where you are at with creating one.

The current reality generally includes the preoccupations of your limited self, your underlying assumptions, thoughts and emotions – it's your perception of how things are. You will really see your underlying assumptions and the strategies that accompany them when you tune into your current reality.

Imagine the big, blank whiteboard in front of you again. Get it really clean and let go of any need to know what you are going to receive. Sit in the vibration of the circle of your current reality. Now summon a symbol that will inform you of your current reality.

Now that you have a symbol, interpret it. Allow yourself to make it up. Keep talking/writing about what you receive based on what's obvious about the symbol. Where are you at with this relationship creation? What are the thoughts, emotions and assumptions that are in your current reality.

Keep your interpretation about you. If you are tempted to interpret your symbol as all your partner's shortcomings, you are on the wrong track. If you receive shortcomings, they are yours!

For those of you who would like further clarification on this process, you can download an example reading at:

http://www.pollyannadarling.com/rraudio.html

When you first do these intuitive exercises, it can be very easy to slip into a mindset where the vision is 'good' and the current reality is 'bad'. It can be tempting to skip the current reality and just connect with your vision. If this is happening for you, know that you are approaching the whole thing from your limited self and doing yourself a great disservice.

From your infinitely creative being nothing is 'good' or 'bad', it just is. It is important to connect to the vision so that you are really clear on what you *truly* want in a relationship. It is just as important to connect with your current reality, because you cannot create what you would truly love in a relationship until you understand and accept your underlying assumptions and strategies, until you are wise to your tricks!

You can use the process described above to tune into anything that you would love to create, not just the relationship of your dreams. The more you practice, the better you will get at tapping into the intuitive realm and interpreting your symbols.

The very action of using your intuition and going beyond thoughts, emotions and assumptions, puts the searchlight clearly on what you would love to create because it is action in favour of your heart.

Resolving Tension

Resist the urge to resolve tension using your intuition. You will more than likely get nonsense.

What do I mean by this? Say you just tuned into the relationship of your dreams. You received an incredible vision of a sensual, delicious partnership with a much younger man/woman with dark hair and blue eyes. You were totally connected at the heart, enjoyed many things together and laughed a lot.

Now you're in terrible tension because you don't know anyone who fits the person you saw in your vision and you can't imagine how you'll meet him/her.

Then you get tempted to use your intuition to tune into *how* or even *where* you are going to meet this dream partner. You will more than likely receive complete rubbish because you are attempting to use your intuition from a deficient place in yourself. That deficiency is based in thoughts and emotions that tell you that you can't have it/do it/be it. You are following the loud and bossy voice of your limited self.

Hanging Out in the Unknown

When you use your intuition, you will often receive information that doesn't make sense, that seems illogical or absurd in the light of your current circumstances, or makes you feel uncomfortable. Learn to live with those feelings of discomfort and tension. They don't mean anything.

You will not know *how* a new and amazing partner is going to appear in your life. You may not know *when* either. You will not necessarily know *how* your relationship is going to transform into one that delights and satisfies you.

Furthermore, when you hang out in the unknown, you are giving yourself the opportunity to receive from the whole of life, not just from your limited idea of what is possible.

> *"If you limit your choices only to what seems possible or reasonable, you disconnect yourself from what you truly want, and all that is left is compromise."*
>
> Robert Fritz

When you think you know *how*, you are limited by what you know from the past and by what you can conceive of. There are vastly more possibilities out there than our minds can come up with.

Once you get used to hanging out in not-knowing, you will learn to love it. It's mysterious, exciting and brimming with possibility. Imagine what *could* happen if you allow your tension to be there and rest in receiving what's possible!

The Power of Choice

If you've come this far in the book, you now have a pretty good idea of what the relationship of your wildest dreams actually looks like and you will have received this information by doing the guided meditation and/or the intuitive technique described earlier. If you have not written anything down yet, do it now.

Write down what you have received about your relationship, capturing in your own words the qualities and essence of that relationship.

Take yourself back to the vibration and qualities of the relationship you would truly love to create. You are now going to create a choice for yourself. Using the words, images and impressions that you received in the intuitive exercises, make up a relationship choice for yourself.

If you are not in a relationship, come up with a choice about creating it. For example, *"I choose to create the relationship of my wildest dreams."*

Don't labour over this – no thinking. Just reconnect with your vision, use the words you have written down and create a choice. Simple is good. Some people like long-winded, wordy choices, but they can be cumbersome in the long run.

Don't worry about getting it exactly right. Your choice is a tool that will connect you to what you truly love. The wording is important – you want the words to connect you to the vibration of what you love – but they are still secondary to using your intuition and receiving your truth.

If you are in a relationship, your choice may look a little different. Here are some real-life examples:

I choose being entwined with Asher in joy, love and passion.

I choose to honour my beautiful wife with a healthy passion.

I choose sharing and exploring experiences through a gentle, loving relationship.

Make sure the wording of the choice connects you to your vision, what you would truly love.

Working with choice sets up a structure in your consciousness that you will use to bring what you love into your life.

"The way to activate the seeds of your creation is by making choices about the results you want to create. When you make a choice, you activate vast human energies and resources, which otherwise go untapped."

Robert Fritz

You have, by now, formulated a choice about your relationship – either about creating one, or transforming the one you are in. You formulated your choice using what you intuitively received about what you would love in a relationship – it's your truth.

The vision of what you would love to create and your current reality around that set up a structure in your consciousness that will compel your vision into being.

One further step is required however – action. You can tune into your vision and current reality for ever and a day and you will not create the relationship you would truly love.

> To create, you must act.

It takes courage to follow your intuition: sometimes the information you receive may not make sense, sometimes you will have thoughts and emotions arising that tell you not to follow what you have received.

Your mind will come up with all kinds of absurd and ridiculous things that you *need* to do to create the relationship of your dreams, like lose ten kilos, buy more clothes, work-out at the gym, hang out in bars, etc. Don't worry about that. You are going to use your intuition to discover what action to take.

Taking Action

It's tempting for many of us to see 'action' as lots of doing. Sometimes you will get action steps that involve 'doing' something. Other times they will be internal actions, like reminding yourself about something or cultivating knowing. Below are some actions people have received to give you an idea of the diversity of the word 'action' in this context.

Action to take, if any:

- Look into his eyes, let the feminine show.
- Relax, loosen up, dig the garden.
- Take care of myself, nurture myself.
- Just be.
- Connect more in innocence with nature.

Using the process described earlier, tune into a vision and current reality for your relationship choice. Write down what you receive.

Now, go back into a state of innocence, letting go of any need to know. Imagine the big, blank whiteboard in front of you. Define another circle around you as 'action to take, if any' to create the relationship of your dreams and summon a symbol that will inform you of what action there is to take, if any.

Now interpret your symbol in the usual way and write down what you receive.

Information received via intuition can be illogical, irrational and unreasonable. You may be tempted to dismiss the 'action' step you received because you can't see how that relates to creating or transforming a relationship. Once again, let any feelings like that be there in your consciousness and do it anyway.

Now you have a complete structure: a vision (the relationship you would love to create), a current reality (how things stand currently in relation to what you would love to create) and an 'action' step.

> Taking your action steps will eventually compel your vision into reality.

If you would truly love to create or transform a relationship, use your intuition to tune into your vision, current reality and action step once every week.

Do your action steps.

Acting in Favour of Your Creation

If every moment of your existence is a creation, then every action you take is an action in favour of creating. The question is, what are you acting in favour of?

Every action you take is an action in favour of something.

Everything you do, everything you say, every thought, every gesture, every breath is all action in favour of something.

When you're complaining to your friend about your partner, your job, your children and all the other things there are to whinge about, you are acting in favour of your underlying assumptions: that you can't have what you want, that you are powerless to change your life, that you can't trust others, that you need to control, etc.

When you are endlessly indulging in thoughts about how annoying your partner is, how selfish they are, how irritating they are, you are acting in favour of your underlying assumption: I'm powerless, I can't have what I want, there is a right way, etc.

When you're picking a fight with your partner because of something they've said, you're acting in favour of your underlying assumptions: I need to control myself (and others and the world), I can't have what I want, etc.

When you're recalling an activity you did with your partner – a dinner, lovemaking, a conversation, an outing – and thinking, *"that sucked, it wasn't how I wanted it"*, you are acting in favour of your underlying assumptions: I'm incapable, I can't, I don't have the capacity, etc.

Ask yourself: *"What did I act in favour of in the last hour, the last day, the last week? What have I acted in favour of for most of my life? In my relationship or when creating a relationship, what do I usually act in favour of? Am I acting in favour of creating an amazing, fulfilling, delicious partnership, or am I acting in favour of everything I don't want?"*

When you act in favour of your underlying assumptions (some of which may be buried as deeply as the Titanic), you are creating your future reality, one which reflects those assumptions more and more strongly: more selfishness and irritation from your partner, more fights, more horrid skin-crawling dates with unsuitable partners, more activities you don't enjoy.

> When you act in favour of your underlying assumptions, you prove them to be 'true'.

Start acting in favour of what you would love to create today, right now, this minute. The relationship you would really love – the one that will bring you true, lasting joy and satisfaction. You know what it looks like, even if you have neglected it for eons.

If you love to cuddle, put the book down right now and go give your partner a cuddle, even if you've just had a fight!

If you'd really love a great relationship, catch yourself when you're thinking about how annoying your partner is, put that to one side (without judging yourself) and shift your focus to what you'd love.

It's easy. Just start noticing what you are acting in favour of and begin acting in favour of the relationship you would love to be living.

It's funny, but tuning in to action to take is also action in favour of creating the relationship of your dreams. When you go ahead and perform the action that you received from the intuitive realm, you are sending a powerful message to your infinite creative being about what you really want to create.

Try it and notice the results over time.

Force Versus Focus

It's not uncommon to attempt to use structure to *control* reality, particularly if your underlying assumptions are 'I'm powerless' or 'I'm not safe'.

The structure of using choice and all of the other techniques in this book are not designed to control outcomes. They are designed to enable you to receive what you would truly love – a blissful, satisfying, fulfilling relationship with another human being.

The techniques I'm presenting do this by shifting the focus of your powerful consciousness from your underlying assumptions, to what you would love to create. This shift requires you to become comfortable with the tension of not knowing what is going to happen, instead of any false sense of security you might derive from believing you have control over your reality.

Being in the mystery of following intuitive guidance is a very different paradigm to one where you believe you are in control of your reality.

Using Choice

What you are doing when you make a choice is saying, *"OK so I know where I'm currently at with this and what my thoughts and emotions are about it. They can be there. However, I'm choosing ..."*

If I have just had a fight with my partner and feel and think evil things about him, I will remind myself of my relationship choice. I acknowledge what I'm thinking and feeling and then refocus on my relationship choice (which is currently: *I choose playful passionate creating with King Asher*).

I'm not trying to force something different. I accept that we just had a fight and I remember it means nothing.

What I'm doing is recognising the voice of my limited self (via my thoughts and emotions) and remembering that I am a divinely creative being and that what I actually want is to continue to create what I love – my delicious relationship with Asher.

> You have the power to choose
> what you create in your relationship.

Owning Your Desires

You may remember earlier in this book I mentioned my own experience of believing that the relationship I truly wanted wasn't possible, not for me, not in this world. I felt embarrassed to even want what I wanted and wouldn't tell anyone about it.

When I began using my intuition to discover what I would love and kept finding that I truly wanted romance and a beautiful wedding, I cringed. My thoughts and emotions told me I was being totally ridiculous, that if people knew what I wanted they would tell me I was dreaming and maybe even laugh at me. Clearly my underlying assumptions had the power.

I flatly refused to share what I received with anyone. Once, I managed to tell (through gritted teeth) one of my very close friends what I wanted. It's ridiculous, but I actually thought I might die just saying it, that's how sure I was that it was absurd.

Why am I telling you this, you may ask? Because if you truly want to create a great relationship (or anything else for that matter), you must own it. I didn't create the relationship of my dreams until I admitted to myself that actually, *yes*, I did really want that, and I took the power out of the underlying assumptions.

You will notice that in my example, when I tuned into what I truly desired, I experienced 'negative' emotions. I didn't want to share my desire. I coach many people who experience the same thing. What they truly desire creates tremendous discomfort, primarily because they don't believe they can have it.

If you follow your 'feelings', which many modalities suggest, you may reject your truth because it makes you feel 'bad', thus depriving yourself of life experiences which will knock your socks off.

You may experience very 'good' feelings when you let go of what you truly desire to create. Now you're off the hook, out of a tight spot, free from those nasty unpleasant feelings of tension.

Your thoughts and emotions do not reflect reality, they reflect your underlying assumptions. If you find yourself feeling discomfort about what you have intuitively received about the relationship you would love to create, acknowledge that those feelings are driven by your underlying assumptions.

It is important to let yourself dream and imagine your relationship dreams as possibility. Acknowledge any stories you are telling yourself about what you would love. Acknowledge any thoughts and emotions that tell you that you can't, or it's not possible, or that your dream is silly. Then take steps to own what you would love to create:

- Tell people about the relationship you would love to create, write it down, draw a picture of it and give it your creative energy.

- Accept what you would love as a possibility (even if your thoughts and emotions are still telling you that it's not).

- Use your intuition as often as you want to and discover more about what you would truly love.

- Ask yourself, if absolutely everything was possible, what would you love your relationship to look like?

- Own your choice as being what you want to create.

The Far Horizon Trap

What you would love is not away somewhere on a distant horizon waiting for you. If you think of the relationship you would truly love as being far away, you will always be moving towards it, but never actually *in* it.

You don't need to pack up your things and settle in for a long journey to Xanadu. More often than not, what you would love is right under your nose or at the furthest, just a few action steps away. The vision of the relationship of your dreams is here with you now, it's simply a matter of creating it.

Practical Choice

Step 1: Connect each day with the relationship choice you created from tuning in to your vision, regardless of how you are 'feeling' about it.

You can do this by writing it down, connecting to the vibration of the choice, imagining what you would love, drawing it, or whatever combination works for you.

Sometimes you will fully experience the vibration of your choice, sometimes you won't. It doesn't matter whether you do or you don't. It's more enjoyable to connect with the vibration of it, but if it doesn't happen, don't worry about it, it won't affect your creation.

Step 2: Once a week, tune into the vision, current reality and action to take for your relationship choice. Take the action you get, even if it doesn't make sense or you don't want to do it.

Step 3: Notice what is appearing in your reality now that you are making your choice.

Step 4: Open yourself to receiving what you would love.

Imagination and Receiving

The role of imagination in creating what you would love cannot be underestimated. It's one of the most powerful tools in your creative toolbox.

Unfortunately, the language of our culture tends to discourage using imagination for anything other than writing stories, penning poems or painting pictures and can be downright negative about it: *"It's all in your imagination,"* or *"You're imagining things,"* and so on.

Your Imagination Amplifies Your Focus

The truth is that when you harness your imagination in favour of what you would love to create, you amplify your creative focus. Your imagination connects you to the realm of infinite possibility.

To create the relationship you would love, you have to be prepared to engage your imagination. For some of us, it's hard to conceive that what we would love is really possible. This is where imagination can really bring life to your creations.

Naturally, you are free to engage your imagination in favour of your underlying assumptions. It's a powerful tool. If you give energy to imagining your partner with someone else, imagining him/her spending all your money, imagining a world full of unsuitable partners, imagining your soul-mate arguing with your parents, imagining him/her spitting fire at you in an argument, you are going to create realities that you don't enjoy.

Your imagination is not discerning.
You can use it for whatever you want.

So, let's look at this premise: your imagination amplifies your focus. Are you focused on what you don't want, or are you focused on what you would love to create?

Your imaginative powers will amplify that focus, rocket boost the power of that focus. The more time and energy you invest in imagining what you would love, the closer that reality becomes and the more connected you are to what you truly want.

Practical Imagination

Step 1: Ask yourself these questions:

1. What would I truly love in a relationship/ partner (an existing one, or one that I want to create)? You should be able to answer this using information supplied by your intuition.

2. Are any of these criteria driven by underlying assumptions? For example, are they responses to your underlying assumptions of powerlessness, or trust, or insignificance? Or are you including something because it's the opposite of what you don't want?

Now imagine yourself in the relationship; imagine your partner. Flesh it all out with details, images, sensory input and description.

Keep your imagining present: that is, when you see it in your mind's eye, don't let it be far away. Stand in your imaginings, your vision. Imagine it as though it's right here now.

You may find that your underlying assumptions will rise up: *"You can't have that,"* or *"That's not possible,"* or *"As if!"* Just let them be there and keep imagining what your heart would truly love.

Step 2: Use your intuitive power to discover action to take towards what you would love. Using the techniques described earlier, put yourself in the circle of 'action to take, if any' towards creating the relationship of your dreams' and receive a symbol that will inform you of that. Then take that action.

Receiving Your Creation

Hooray! Now you know what your underlying assumptions are and how to neutralise them. You know the delicious relationship you would love to create and you've already started using the techniques in this book to begin creating it. That's wonderful.

Now, you must receive what you're creating. We humans are very weird – we know what we would love, but often it can be jumping up and down in front of us, shouting our name and waving bright red flags and *still* we don't see it.

When I met my partner (the man that does it for me on every level, with whom I have an amazing creative partnership), I tried to push him away.

Through intuitive exercises I had discovered that I would love romance, a partner in creating, great sex and a beautiful marriage (I've already mentioned my aversion to that!!). Then one Saturday, I went to a party painted gold and met Asher. I recognised him intuitively as exactly what I wanted as soon as I met him, but my searchlight was firmly trained on my assumptions. My thoughts and emotions were generally 'negative' about being in a relationship, and for months I floundered around trying to avoid him.

Following intuitive guidance, I went home with Asher on that Saturday, something I would *never* normally do. This created huge discomfort in me, even though we had a wonderful time together. The next day we had more fun, but the loud voice of my limited self was screaming streams of freaked-out nonsense in my head.

For a good six months, I completely failed to receive the relationship of my wildest dreams. I wallowed around in my assumptions that I wasn't good enough and unlovable and all the stories that go with them (like who wants a mother of three with an angry ex-husband?).

I avoided true intimacy with a man who was ready and willing to give me everything I always secretly dreamed about.

It sounds mad, but it often happens. You may have spent most of your life *not* receiving what you would love. Perhaps sometimes you do, but in a haphazard and unreliable way that you can't repeat because you don't know how you did it!

This is not because of the whim of the gods. It's because you are not aligned with what you truly love – you are not allowing your expanded boundless, limitless, creative self to give you exactly what you would dearly love.

To receive the relationship of your dreams you have to be ready and willing to embrace your creation.

That means, when someone shows up in your reality who is in line with what you already know you would love to create, you have to give him/her the opportunity to make your heart sing. If an amazing, fascinating woman appears in your life and you reject her because her nose is too big or because she's too old or she has a weird job, you are on a long and lonely road.

Furthermore, you may already have a partner who, on some level, is in line with everything you love, but you let your assumptions and stories get in the way of receiving the true depth of your relationship. If this is the case, you are going to have to come to terms with letting the stories go and with actually receiving the true beauty of your connection.

Asher, the man of my dreams, is nine years younger than me. Good reason for me to reject him. And I tried. You have no idea what a fuss my limited self made when he began to tell me what year he was born. I heard *"Nineteen eighty..."*. As soon as the 'eight' was out of his mouth, I wigged out. *"What! He's younger than me. That's not OK. Eek. Help."* Blah blah, you know how it goes.

I wanted to run away right then and there. Irrational and ridiculous, but true and common.

I told myself bucket loads of tall tales about the age difference. They served really well in stopping me from receiving my creation – the relationship of my wildest dreams. Once I got over myself and relaxed into receiving, I was truly astonished by the depth of passion, intimacy and love that I found myself in.

So how do you do this? How do you receive this amazing relationship?

You have to plunge into the unknown.

That's right, no one is going to hand you a piece of paper telling you where the relationship is going. That's up to you. No one is going to offer to hold your hand (except maybe this possible partner bursting with potential). You have to bravely go into the great wilds of not knowing what will happen or how it's going to turn out, where no man/woman has gone before!

It may be scary, it may freak you out, it may not turn out the way you expected, but I'm here to tell you that it's totally worth it.

One of the most beautiful things about creating in this way is that you always receive more than you imagined. I had never even conceived of the intense, extraordinary energetic connection that I share with my partner.

When you open to receiving the relationship you would truly love, you will find that your infinite creative being can create vastly more delights than you dreamed possible!

Timing

There is no knowing *when* you will create what you love. It could be in six months, but it might also be tomorrow! This may not be in line with your thinking. I certainly wasn't 'ready' for the amazing relationship that I created in my reality.

Be prepared to receive, even if the timing seems wrong or the circumstances unlikely.

Practical Receiving

Know that if you are putting energy into creating what you would love, it will show up at some point.

Be open to receiving your creation. This means being vulnerable to your fears and freak outs.

Know that you won't know!!! You will not know where it's going or how things will end up.

Continue using the tools and techniques in this book to keep putting the power of your consciousness into what you would love to create. Take action towards that.

> "Imagination is more important than knowledge. For knowledge is limited to all we now know and understand, while imagination embraces the entire world, and all there ever will be to know and understand."
>
> Albert Einstein

PART 5

Transforming Your Existing Relationship

Transforming Your Existing Relationship

If you are not in a relationship, you may be tempted to skip this chapter! I won't be offended, but you will be doing yourself a great disservice. In particular, you will miss out on using your intuition to discover your true nature and essence.

The model *It's All You* assumes that you have the power to transform your existing relationship. You can train your searchlight on what you want to create in the relationship.

Whether you are aware of it or not, until now you have been making demands on your partner (consciously or unconsciously). You will have been seeking approval, validation, power and control, trust, love, or any combination of these, and expecting your partner to fulfill your demands.

"Oh I never make demands like that of my partner!" you might say. Some people demand out loud, others energetically, others via certain behaviours, for example testing their partner to see if they can be trusted, or creating drama in

order to gain control in the relationship. Whatever the method, these demands are made, even in the most enlightened relationship.

The truth is, that you will always be tempted to make such demands. After all, you've been doing it since you arrived in the world and first began relationships with your parents (or care givers).

This chapter is not about everything that's wrong with your current relationship or you, it's not about fixing or changing, it's about *shifting the power of your consciousness into what you would love to create.*

The first step on that path is to acknowledge and understand the current reality of your relationship.

Your Current Relationship Reality

Where were you coming from within yourself when you originally created your relationship? This is a great question to ask yourself as it will show you what you are primarily focused on in your relationship.

Generally people come together for two main reasons:

1. Because they are unconsciously attempting to resolve their tension around feelings of incompleteness – seeking a significant other who will complete them; or

2. Because they are consciously or unconsciously fulfilling a heartfelt desire to create loving partnership with another human being.

Your response to the question just gives you the current reality of your relationship, it means nothing about what you can create from here. If you have been in your relationship for a significant amount of time (over five years), you are unlikely to have a clear view to your original motivation for creating the relationship. Luckily that's not important!

Regardless of why you originally created your relationship, it is possible to transform it. The level of energy required from you depends on how deeply entrenched and attached you are to the unspoken egoic waltz that you play out with your partner.

In other words, *how attached are you to all the crap in your relationship?*

"Ooh!" I hear you howl in outrage, *"I am not attached to my relationship crap, I hate it."* But truthfully, at some level, you *love* it. (See 'Awareness of Your Addictions', page 67.)

Let's get some insight into your current relationship reality.

Answer all of the questions below. Your focus will naturally drift when you are without a clear concept of what you would love to create. Your answers reveal your default preoccupations.

Note: It is incredibly important that you are honest about the answers. Never mind how awful they sound, or how politically incorrect they are, or what you think they mean about you, *be brutally honest.* These answers are for your eyes only.

The more honest, upfront and non-judgmental you can be about your thoughts and emotions, the further along the road to transforming your relationship you will travel.

Include *everything.* There are no right or wrong answers.

1. List *all* of the major problems in your relationship.

2. List *everything* you don't like about your partner (absolutely everything, even really stupid things like, *"I don't like the way she says Hi,"* or *"I don't like his yellow toenails,"* or *"I hate the way he always leaves his towel on the bathroom floor"*).

3. List *everything* you do like about your partner.

4. List *all* the improvements you would like to see in your relationship. List everything no matter how stupid or inconsequential it seems.

5. What is your role in the relationship? Write down whatever answer comes to you first.

Take a look at the real-life example below:

List all of the major problems in your relationship.
Communication, shared labour, intimacy, money, parenting style.

List everything you don't like about your partner.
Messy, self absorbed, doesn't listen, leaves shower messy, not enough clothes, effeminate, quick to anger, bad driver, slow to respond (slow communicator), tight with money, doubts himself constantly, unworldly (not a lot of experience with worldly things), a bit naive, hate that he forgets birthdays.

List everything you do like about your partner.
Creative, intelligent, adventurous spirit, cooks well, great sense of style, gives really good massages, sensitive, can tell him anything (can be open), he loves the outdoors (nature), makes me laugh, we love playing games together, he knows things I don't – I learn from him, love the way he looks aesthetically.

List all the improvements you would like to see in your relationship.
More shared time together, more time, more money, both of us to be doing what we love, we need a focus (a personal one and a shared one), would like him to be more engaged

in the household and more forthcoming in contributing, would like him to be more generous with his energy, would like to trust more and be more relaxed in the flow of life, would like to receive him more, would like to cook together more, would like him to communicate his feelings more (share rather than project), want us to be able to enjoy this time rather than be in angst and constant working out, time for us (the two of us – intimate time).

What is your role in the relationship? Write down whatever answer comes to you first.
Mother.

All of the above comprise the respondent's *perception* of the relationship, perceived from their limited self. The answers are based on thoughts and emotions about the relationship – the limited self's way of perceiving reality.

You will notice that improvements desired all come from a place of lack and deficiency, ie. they are all based on things that the respondent believes they don't currently have. This question is included to reveal what you focus on when you are engaged in your relationship through the veil of your perceptions.

You have two ways to function within your relationship: with your searchlight wildly jumping from one underlying assumption to another; or with it firmly trained on what you would love to create.

Without an expanded concept of what you would truly love in a relationship, your focus will naturally default to rest with the answers you have given to these questions, whether you are aware of it or not. You don't need much imagination to conceive of the day-to-day reality that this focus creates.

Take a look at the answers you've given to the questions. Which aspects are you primarily focused on? What is your general perception of your partner – the person you have described in question 1 or the one in question 2?

Tall Tales

There is a story (or several stories) that you tell yourself and others about your partner, your relationship and yourself. These stories mask your underlying assumptions and reinforce the reality you are creating in your relationship. They are usually your attempts to resolve the tension you have about your relationship reality.

You will be very attached to these stories and convinced that they are real.

> Remember, you are a powerful creative being, you are creating every minute of your existence, consciously or unconsciously.

The stories that you tell yourself and others contribute to your relationship reality, reinforce it, add detail and create focus. By listening to what you tell yourself and others about your partner, your relationship and yourself, you will see what you are primarily focused on and easily deduce the reality you are creating.

Take a look at the responses to the questions on pages 149–150. The person involved has stories about:

- her partner being self absorbed and not helping with the household and parenting;
- the relationship lacking communication and intimacy; and
- herself as a martyred mother figure who does all the work.

Picture the day to day reality that repeating these stories to herself and others will create for her – lots of resentment, withdrawal, anger and heaviness.

Your ability to let go of your stories about the relationship and your partner determines your ability to transform your relationship. You may find yourself quite attached to the stories, they're a bit like a security blanket for an infant – they define your reality and keep you safely in a known realm, even if it's one that often sucks, and just like that blanket, gets old and smelly!

Listen to what you tell others about your partner and your relationship. Listen to the voice in your head when you are in conflict with your partner. What is it saying about you, them and the relationship?

Hear it and then disregard it. It's nonsense, designed to hold you in a paradigm that will not serve you. It takes time to truly let them go, but when you hear yourself telling tales, listen, acknowledge that you are limiting your possibilities and then dismiss them.

When you let go of your habitual stories about your partner, the relationship and yourself, you create space in your consciousness for what you would truly love to become a reality.

Defining Reality

The way that you define your partner and your relationship make a tremendous difference to the way you experience your relationship reality.

No one likes to admit that they think crappy things about their partner, but *everyone* does it. Your definitions connect you to your imagination and change your experience and emotions.

For example, if I'm feeling grouchy and uptight and get focused on how my partner is, I might start thinking that he's very controlling. There's my definition: he's controlling.

My imagination immediately picks up that definition and runs with it. In no time at all, I actually experience a difference in the way Asher looks and sounds. Suddenly his voice is angry and forceful, his features ugly and contorted by his vicious controlling nature! My emotions run high, I feel angrier and more antagonistic towards him. I find him unattractive.

It's total garbage by the way! He hasn't changed. Nothing has actually changed except my definition.

When I'm connected to what I love, I define Asher as my king. He's tall, handsome, big-hearted, magical and supportive. By the way, that is not affirmative polarising, it's what I know to be true through using my intuition.

I don't always experience the truth of my partner and neither will you. Your experience (and consequently your emotions) will change with your definitions. You will create a more satisfying experience if you connect with the truth of your partner. Naturally, there is an intuitive process that will connect you to that truth.

Next time you hear your inner voice ranting away about your partner, ask yourself, *"How am I defining my partner? What are they?"* Be honest when you reply, don't haze over it with positive waffle.

Then ask, *"Is that what I would love to create and receive?"*

Be aware, also, of the way you are defining the relationship. In long-term relationships, it's easy to fall into habitual ways of defining. For example, I consistently viewed my previous marriage as dysfunctional. Whenever I thought about it, or talked about it, that was how I defined it. Consequently, I felt hopeless about it and the reality in the marriage was dismal.

Relationship definitions driven by underlying assumptions create enormous tension which many people are tempted to resolve by discussing the state of the relationship. This is entirely pointless, as your definitions aren't real. You made them up!

If you find yourself in terrible tension about the relationship itself, have a look at how you are defining it. Allow your limited definitions to be there in your consciousness and know that they are not real. Resist the temptation to resolve your tension.

Shifting the Focus to What You Love

By now you will be well-acquainted with the current status of your existing relationship. If you're reading this book, it's likely that you are unsatisfied with that relationship for some reason. You will have discovered a lot about yourself and the way that you've created that relationship. Now it's time to refocus on what you truly want to create.

The most powerful thing that you can do to create the relationship of your wildest dreams is this:

> When your relationship is in trouble, there's conflict or you're feeling crappy about your partner, acknowledge what it's about for *you* (which underlying assumptions have the power) and then imagine what you would love.

Reconnect with your relationship choice (see 'The Power of Choice', page 119). Use your imagination to stand in that choice and see it as though it already exists and then *take action* towards that choice.

Your action steps may not always be easy to take. Remember, you are very attached to your crappy thoughts and emotions, to your position on 'how it is'. You may not 'feel' like taking action towards what you would love to create. Do it anyway. Notice the results.

The Truth About Your Partner

As far as the relationship experience goes *It's All You* – remember the model. So who is this person, your partner?

At this point you may be lured into circular thinking such as, *"Well if it's all me, does my partner actually exist at all?"* You can go there if you want to, but it's a waste of your energy. There is no answer to that question or others like it and anyone who says they have one has just made it up!

Stay with me on this. Once again I'm asking you to assume that what I am presenting is true and experiment with it. Notice the changes that take place. Do not get sidetracked by metaphysical querying! It won't get you any closer to creating a wildly satisfying, delicious relationship.

So what *do* we know about your partner? Firstly, your partner is an infinite, divinely creative being, just like you. As an infinite creative being, they also have a limited self, characterised by their underlying assumptions and the thoughts, emotions and behaviours that go with them.

It is likely that you are very familiar with what you perceive to be your partner's faults and shortcomings – their limited self. You have probably been focused on these shortcomings, consciously or unconsciously, for much of the relationship.

The true nature of your partner's expanded being will be less familiar, but you will have experienced it at some time (usually the beginning of the relationship), even if you are not aware of it.

Seeing and experiencing your partner's true nature allows you to redefine your relationship reality and to connect with what you love. It also gives you something to refocus on when you've drifted back to your default focus, your underlying assumptions.

Like I said, you may already be aware of your partner's true nature, their essential expanded essence. If not, don't worry about it. Even if you are aware of it, you can always deepen your connection to that.

How? By modifying the intuitive techniques you have already learned in this book. You are going to tune into your partner's true nature and expanded essence.

But before you do that, we're going to discover *your* true nature and expanded essence. Some people love doing this, others find it ghastly. For many people discovering how amazing they are is much more painful than discovering their shortcomings!

Whatever your response to doing this, engage your backbone and do it anyway.

Audio Guidance

To be guided through this process, you can download the audio file *"Who is this person anyway? A: Me"* at:

http://www.pollyannadarling.com/rraudio.html

Otherwise, follow the instructions below.

Your True Nature and Expanded Essence

Firstly, read through all the instructions before you begin so you don't have to keep referring to them and disrupt your intuitive flow.

What you receive about yourself may come as symbols or literally. For example, every time I tune into my true nature and expanded essence, I'm flying above the earth (often as an eagle, sometimes as Eva from the Pixar movie *Wall-E*!) and can see absolutely everything. The vibration is of freedom and clarity, and an enhanced intuitive ability. That's an interpretation. I'm not actually an eagle or Eva!

The more you do this process, the deeper you will connect with your true nature. You may not believe it, you may feel uncomfortable, you may feel wonderful. What you believe and feel makes no difference and doesn't matter. What matters is that you connect to the truth.

Be open to what you receive. If what you get is very obviously a symbol, use the discipline of interpreting not describing.

Sometimes you may experience enjoyable emotions when you connect to your true nature. This is nice, but not essential. If you don't feel emotionally connected to what you get, don't worry about it. It's not necessary to feel emotionally connected to discover the truth.

Find a space and time where you won't be disturbed.

Sit in a comfortable position and uncross your arms and legs.

If you have a lot of resistance to doing this process, acknowledge that now.

Choose to serve your heart.

Choose to be in innocence, let go of any need to know and anything you think you already know. Imagine a completely blank whiteboard in front of you.

Define a circle in front of you as your true nature and expanded essence.

Begin to imagine that circle vibrating with this true nature and expanded essence.

Once the circle is humming with vibration, imagine stepping into it.

Choose to receive the essence and qualities of your expanded true nature.

Allow those qualities to come to you. If you have to wait a while, that's OK.

Notice the vibration of your true nature and expanded essence. Notice any talents or abilities that support that.

Once you have strongly connected to this essence, write it down.

Keep stepping back into the circle of your true nature and expanded essence and ask, *"What else?"* Write down any further information you receive and interpret any symbols.

Well, that's you done. Now for your partner.

If You Are Not Currently in a Relationship

If you are making your relationship choice and are open to receiving, sooner or later a potential partner will show up in your reality. You may like him/her immediately, you may not.

No matter how long you have known this person or what you feel about him/her, you can use the technique below to tune into their true nature and expanded essence and discover a dimension of their being that you otherwise might never experience.

You can also use this process to discover the true nature and expanded essence of an ex-partner. This is an enjoyable and enlightening experience!

Your Partner's True Nature and Expanded Essence

Firstly, read through all the instructions before you begin so you don't have to keep referring to them and disrupt your intuitive flow.

What you receive about your partner may come as symbols or literally. For example, every time I tune into my partner's true nature and expanded essence, I see a huge mountain with a vast base. The vibration is of strength and grounded power, support and great stillness at the core. That's an interpretation. Obviously, he isn't actually a mountain!

Be open to what you receive. If what you get is very obviously a symbol, use the discipline of interpreting not describing.

Sometimes you may experience enjoyable emotions when you connect to your partner's true nature. This is nice, but not essential. If you don't feel emotionally connected to what you get, don't worry about it. It's not necessary to feel emotionally connected to discover the truth.

Audio Guidance

To be guided through this process, you can download the audio file *"Who is this person anyway? B: Partner"* at:

http://www.pollyannadarling.com/rraudio.html

Otherwise, follow the instructions below.

Find a space and time where you won't be disturbed.

Sit in a comfortable position and uncross your arms and legs.

Choose to serve your heart.

If you are experiencing any resistance to discovering your partner's true nature and expanded essence, acknowledge it at this point.

Choose to be in innocence, let go of any need to know and anything you think you already know. Imagine a completely blank whiteboard in front of you.

Define a circle in front of you as your partner's true nature and expanded essence.

Begin to imagine that circle vibrating with this true nature and expanded essence.

Once the circle is humming with vibration, imagine stepping into it.

Choose to receive the essence and qualities of your partner's expanded true nature. Allow those qualities to come to you. If you have to wait a while, that's OK.

Notice the vibration of your partner's true nature and expanded essence. Notice any talents or abilities that support that.

Once you have strongly connected to their essence, write it down.

Keep stepping back into the circle of your partner's true nature and expanded essence and ask, *"What else?"* Write down any further information you receive and interpret any symbols.

Truth and Definition

Seeing and/or experiencing the true nature and expanded essence of your partner (and other people) is an incredibly powerful tool that will transform your relationships. When you know a person's true nature, you cannot continue to define them only by their limited self.

Seeing someone's true nature redefines them in your reality, changes the definition in your imagination and revolutionises your experience.

Seeing your own true nature and expanded essence is amazingly powerful. No longer are you solely defined by your underlying assumptions, thoughts and emotions. There is another dimension to your being, one that you can freely access via your intuition. You may not believe what you have received. You don't need to. Assume that it's true, act as if it's true, notice the changes in your reality.

As far as relationships go, knowing your own and your partner's true nature and expanded essence can be a very useful tool in determining suitability and understanding basic relationship dynamics.

In our true, expanded nature, Asher and I are well suited. His grounded strength balances my soaring freedom, his deep stillness is a perfect foil to my wildness. We are compatible and complimentary in our infinite beings. We are also nicely matched in our limited selves!

Connecting with your partner's true nature and expanded essence will also cultivate admiration, affection, wonder and awe in you – all of which are useful in creating a fulfilling relationship reality!

Happily Ever After

So you've created a blissful, satisfying relationship with the partner of your dreams, or maybe you've transformed a tired, drooping relationship into a sizzling romantic ride. Now what?

Once the glow and novelty of the new has faded and you're into the humdrum of everyday life, how do you keep the romance alive?

Firstly, forget that question. It's a much colluded-upon story in our culture that relationships are magical and beautiful in the first flush and then they become numbed out and dulled by time, until they eventually fall into total disrepair. Unless of course, you happen to be one of the 'lucky few' couples who 'really work at it'. Hogwash!

A relationship does not require work. There is no reason for it to fall into a dismal heap unless you want it to.

An amazing relationship requires creativity and a commitment to what you love. That's all.

Create or Surrender

The unadorned truth is that if you stop creating the relationship the way you would love it, you will inevitably fall into the preoccupations of your limited self.

Without commitment to what you would love to create, your focus will drift back to your underlying assumptions, leaving you wondering *"why is it always like this?"* etc. If you have done any of the exercises in this book, you know where this will take you – to an unenjoyable, predictable reality where the relationship slowly goes wrong until one or both of you either call it quits or sink into a mire of uninspired, depressing daily life.

Even the most inspired and passionate relationships can become drab and disconnected. If you are not putting your creative energy into it, you will just default to creating from your underlying assumptions.

> When you take your inspired, creative energy out of your relationship, you inevitably become lured into the preoccupations of your limited self.

Though you may initially recognise the stories you are telling yourself as being those of your limited self, if you continue to withhold your creative energy from the relationship, over time you will come to believe that those same stories actually represent reality.

Here's the beautiful truth - you can rediscover the magic and intimacy that you originally created in your relationship.

> It's never too late to put your focus on what you truly love.

That's right. It's never too late to pull the pin on the strategies and addictions. You can do this at any time and transform your creation. It may not turn out the way you expect, but you will always end up with what you love, one way or another.

Vulnerability

Dropping all the stories you tell yourself about your relationship and your partner will mean that you are vulnerable to the unknown. These stories provide a psychological barrier that protects your heart and blocks your ability to see the truth. Without them, you are vulnerable to the unknown. You won't know what is going to happen.

It takes courage to be vulnerable in this way. You obviously have barrel loads of courage, or you wouldn't be reading this book! You will find yourself in your relationship in a way that you have never experienced before and it might feel uncomfortable or frightening.

You are handing over the job of lighthouse keeper to your unlimited, boundless creative self. Wonders await you if you can allow that vulnerability.

Forget Perfect

What is the point of this book? It's to facilitate transformation in you that will free you to create the relationship of your dreams. Does that mean that once you have created it, everything will be perfect? No, not a chance.

If your goal is to live a perfect life, with the perfect person in perfect harmony, you are on a very hard road. Good luck with that.

It's a commonly held belief that personal development work will mean that nothing nasty, uncomfortable, depressing, sad or awful will ever happen again. That you will cruise swimmingly through the rest of your days and nights like a Bodhisattva.

The only reason you would want a perfect life is if you are listening to your underlying assumptions and are afraid of conflict and other 'bad' things. You've read this far – you have nothing to fear.

Your 'stuff' will still rise up and you will 'feel' uncomfortable. You will still experience so called 'negative' emotions. You will still have arguments. You will still hear a little voice in your head telling you idiotic stories about your partner and your relationship. You are a human being and life is a wild ride with a wonderful array of experiences to explore.

The great news is that, once you have read to the end of this book, done the exercises and experimented with the model *It's All You*, those 'negative' experiences will have nowhere near their old power to knock you down and trash your relationship. You are on a road to freedom and joy.

If you truly desire a wonderful, nourishing relationship that you value for its own sake, forget about it being perfect. Accept that at times, you will inevitably have your focus on your underlying assumptions and that you will create scenarios that you don't like (by now these will be very familiar to you). Accept that if you do, *it doesn't matter a fig!!!*

That's right. It truly doesn't matter.

> If you find yourself in a reality created by your underlying assumptions, engage your backbone, acknowledge your addictions and refocus on what you truly love.

When you do, you will continually be amazed and delighted by the delicious relationship that you are creating and receiving.

Know Yourself (here it is again!!)

I am unable to tell you what will come up for you in your relationship. If you commit to knowing yourself (what you would love as well as the false paths your limited self would lead you down) and listen to the quiet voice of your heart, you will be able to refocus on what you would love to create without great difficulty. You will begin to recognise your attempts to sabotage your creations and will cultivate the courage to move past them.

Practical Relationship Transformation

Here are some tips for continuing to create what you love in your relationship:

- Every day bring your attention to your vision and choice for your relationship (what you love) and choose it.

- When you find yourself in conflict with your partner, as soon as practical, withdraw and find out what's really going on for *you*, then refocus.

- Never collude with others about aspects of your relationship or your partner that you think are flawed, faulty or need improving – you are buying into your underlying assumptions and assigning them the power of your consciousness. If you're telling yourself a negative story about your partner/ relationship, run yourself through the conflict process on pages 59–60.

- If you have bad relationship days or even weeks, do not beat yourself up about it. Write them off as an accidental foray into your limited self. Then find out what's going on for you, engage your backbone and refocus on your vision.

- Take action towards what you would love to create.

- Listen to the quiet intuitive voice of your heart. If your intuition says put your arm around your partner and your limited self is screaming at you to say something biting and nasty, listen to your intuition. Cultivate your capacity to follow your intuition.

- Cultivate your willingness and ability to be vulnerable to not knowing what will happen.
- Consciously notice the difference in your relationship through your use of these practices. Make a note of what you notice.
- Celebrate and appreciate your power as a creator and enjoy your creation.

It's very simple: you either put your creative energy into creating the relationship you love every day of your life, or you fall prey to the preoccupations of your limited self. You choose.

Children

Creating a child (or several of them) is one of the most extraordinary journeys you can go on in life, a trip that will challenge, frustrate, amaze and inspire you. For many people the desire to create a child arises naturally once they have established a relationship.

I could write a whole book on this topic alone! Presented below is a summary of what's possible in your relationship when you have children according to the model in this book – *It's All You.*

Like everything else in life, a child is either an

opportunity to create what you would love or a ticket to misery.

Unfortunately many relationships go to pot when people have children. Contrary to common belief, this is not because it's inevitable that children put strain on the relationship, or come between the parents, or any one of the tired old stories that do the rounds.

> You can keep creating the relationship you love come what may, hell or high water. It's always your choice.

The only reason children can mess things up is if you create that.

Here's a great example – mine! I was six years into my marriage by the time I had my first child. I had already withdrawn most of my creative energy from the relationship (without understanding what I was doing) and was completely caught in the misery of the stories I told myself about my partner and the relationship.

We fought often, made love very rarely and lived in a kind of domestic stalemate with occasional bursts of happiness. Mostly I felt numb and powerless to change my situation.

I didn't know why it was like that or how I could get out of it. I knew I loved my husband but somehow couldn't get things to turn out the way I wanted. I had some ideas about what I would love, but no idea how to make it happen.

Having my son was a completely wonderful, amazing and life-changing experience. It also gave me ample excuses to stay well away from my husband: baby needs feeding, baby needs to be carried, too tired to make love. In a scenario where I was already looking for excuses to avoid intimacy, driven by an underlying assumption that I would be violated and couldn't trust my partner, a child was an absolute boon, a never ending source of division.

In our case it was never a source of open conflict. We both just accepted that my withdrawal to tend to the child was completely natural and as it should be. Many people will tell you this is true – one of the hard-wired stories we all have going on. Complete nonsense of course. It suited the agenda of my limited self. It was perfect and everyone I spoke to about it bemoaned that that was just 'how it is'.

Do not get sucked into this kind of story, to be blunt - it's bullshit.

I say all this with the benefit of what I know now. At the time, I was at the mercy of my underlying assumptions, knew very little about myself and thought that 'things just happen'.

Beware the Stories

There are lots of stories and no shortage of people who will collude with you about how true they are. One of the most insidious is the 'time for me' story. It goes something like this:

"Well, we have children now so we're not doing anything for ourselves. Our lives are not our own, we're devoted to the children. Therefore, we need time to do our own thing, otherwise we might lose ourselves. Therefore, you (my partner) need to take the child(ren) while I go and do something for myself. Then we'll need to make time for you to do something for yourself. And it has to be equal or we'll get resentful. After that we'll organise time for us and then maybe we'll fit in some family time."

This is all story – the Competing for Energy Game. It's nonsense and it's a trap. Your whole life is your own, you are living it for yourself. You are choosing your life and what you create, including your children.

If you buy into this story, you will cultivate a competition for energy. You and your partner will compete for the available time, each believing that you are entitled to 'time' for yourself. Then you'll try to schedule in 'family time' and then 'time for us'. You'll send yourself mad!

It's a set-up, born from the idea that your life is not your own, that you are a victim of circumstance and of others, and that there is limited time available and it needs to be apportioned. None of which bears any relation to reality.

It's thoughts and emotions stuff and you know where they arise from – yep, underlying assumptions!

Being focused in this way will kill your passion for your partner and hook you into the patterns of your limited self.

The only response is to dismiss the story. If you're focused on what you would love to create, none of the stories matter. In fact when you are creating what you would love, there is always time for everyone.

Here are a few of the other sneaky stories doing the rounds that generate beastly psychological tension that begs to be resolved:

- the children come first, the relationship second;
- the children come first, my needs are secondary; and
- having children means there's no time for my partner and I to be intimate.

Again, these and other similar stories that you might come up with are just that – stories. They do not reflect reality.

There is absolutely no reason on earth why a child should do anything to a relationship other than enrich it – if you create it that way. It's all too easy to slip into using children overtly, covertly or otherwise, to push the agenda of your limited self and trash your relationship.

Weaving Children into Your Creation

Your children are sustained by your loving relationship. That means the relationship comes first, the children second. Ooh, I hear people jumping up and down and saying *"No, no the children have to come first."* It's not true.

If you create an amazing, loving relationship that you value highly, your children will be nourished by it. The children are the product of that loving relationship, even if you have a blended family and live with children that are not biologically yours.

You created the relationship, you created your partner in your life and if they came with children, those children are a part of your creation and can be cherished as such. You may need to have a look at how you are defining them. *It's All You* – remember.

In Summary

- Commit to seeing your stories about your partner and the relationship. See them for what they are – stories that keep you from receiving what is truly available to you.
- Let go of your definitions of your partner.
- Use conflict with your partner as an opportunity to learn more about your assumptions and stories.
- Commit to seeing both yourself and your partner in your true nature and expanded essence.
- Apply everything you have already discovered in this book to family life. *It's All You –* remember!

PART 6

Sex, Lovemaking and Myth

Sex, Lovemaking and Myth

How could a relationship book not include a chapter on that most wonderful pleasure of life? Actually there's not a huge amount to say about it – we all know how to do it! However, as with everything in relationships, there are two ways to approach sex and lovemaking: from your limited self and from your infinite creative being.

Sex and the Limited Self

Mmmm, sex from your limited underlying assumptions. Sounds great doesn't it! Sex is often a battleground in relationships, an easy route to resolve the tension of underlying assumptions by either withholding altogether or by resolving tension through (or during) sexual activity.

If you are in the grips of an underlying assumption, you may be very tempted to use lovemaking as a way to resolve your tension:

- to assert your power by withholding sex;
- to control your partner;

- to express your resentment;
- to prove to yourself that you are unappealing;
- to try and get love;
- to prove that you are not enough (through performance problems).

Whether you're in a serious relationship or not, if the power of your consciousness is focused on your underlying assumptions, you will have an unsatisfying sexual experience with your partner.

Your underlying assumptions can have enormous power in the sexual arena because sex requires intimacy and vulnerability, two things that your limited self is averse to.

The power of your consciousness may be heavily invested in your underlying assumptions as a way of protecting your heart from violation.

Anytime you have an unfulfilling sexual experience, you can guarantee that your focus was on an underlying assumption.

Lovemaking from Your Infinite Creative Being

Without wanting to sound as though there's a 'right way' to make love, there is an amazing, fulfilling life of sexual loving to be had when you receive it from your truth.

That's a ridiculous sounding sentence, but it's true. Imagine right now the divine sex you could have if you're connected strongly to what you truly desire, if you're connected strongly to your true nature and expanded essence – a limitless creative being who would love to connect with a partner in glorious sexual union. *"Yum"* and *"Yes please"* to that.

Whatever stuff you may have around sex, this boundless, creative, infinite being that you truly are, is always accessible to you, in every moment of your existence.

Maybe you already have a great sex life and are saying to yourself *"This doesn't apply to me, I don't have any stuff around sex, my sex life is already fantastic."* That's awesome, but I guarantee that if you enquire within, your heart could expand deeper into your sexual experiences with your partner and lead you to more magical places.

It's worth pointing out, that the amazing lovemaking available to you is not 'movie sex.' You know the kind – Glenn Close and Michael Douglas did it in *Fatal Attraction* – all huffing and puffing, posturing and endlessly inventive ways of doing it. That stuff is all about the 'how': how you do it, where you do it, etc.

There's nothing wrong with it (and you may enjoy it enormously). However it's not actually necessary to romp around the house/elevator/garden/mall in order to have amazing sex!

When you are truly connected to what you would love, it doesn't matter where you are, what you're wearing, how you do it, who does what – you have an extraordinary sexual experience anyway.

There's a whole world of different 'hows' out there if you want to explore them – tantric sex being an example. If you stay connected with what you truly would love to create with your partner, the 'how' is just part of the game. You will be satisfied and delighted.

Practical Sexual Magic

When you have unsatisfying sexual experiences for whatever reason (eg. you felt awful, your focus was elsewhere, your partner smelled bad, etc.) ask yourself these two questions:

1. Where was your focus?
2. Did you have a vision of what you would truly love?

Be honest with yourself. If your experience was crappy, your focus will have been on one of your underlying assumptions.

For now, in this transformational stage of your relationships, make a habit of choosing what you would truly love from your lovemaking. Would you love great sex, deep connection, joy, fun, sensual delight? Ask yourself what you would truly love.

This may change each time, but check in with yourself beforehand and rest in that vision. If other stuff comes up for you, acknowledge it and then take action towards your vision.

For example, say you'd love to create deep connection with your partner, but you feel fearful and guarded. Acknowledge your fear (and whatever assumption it's driven by) and then take action, like breathing into your heart centre and opening to your partner.

It may take practice at the beginning and feel awkward, but eventually you will be so connected to what you would truly love from your lovemaking, that you will automatically focus on the vision and a world of delicious sexual experience will be yours.

Incidentally, outrageous though it may seem, you do not need to ask your partner what they would truly love (I'm outraged just writing it, but it's true). If you choose a state of innocence and ask what you would truly love and go for that, miraculously (and deliciously in this case), your partner will also receive what they would love.

When you follow and act on your true vision, everyone gets what they want!

Creating Myth

Mythology gives us a guiding framework for what takes place in our lives. You can use it to create a context that will serve you in creating the relationship of your dreams. The mythological context that you use for yourself and your significant other can make a substantial difference to what you create.

I am going to talk about the sacred union of masculine and feminine in a mythological context, at the risk of upsetting those of you who are in same sex relationships, or want to create one. If that is you, you can either view this next section literally (and potentially get annoyed!) or you can view it as a metaphor – symbolic of the creative possibilities in your own life.

Sacred Union, Sacred Balance

Many of the ancient cultures of the world have a mythology around the sacred union of masculine and feminine – Yin/Yang, Shiva/Shakti, Jesus/ Mary Magdalen for example. These unions are inspiring and meaningful on many levels and add another dimension to the way that you perceive your relationships.

The union of opposites – the vessel and the blade (the star of David) – represents sacred harmony. The union of masculine and feminine creates life, without it there is no life. This union creates perfect balance.

Within each male there is a masculine and feminine aspect, the same is true for each female. Each is complete, yet unbalanced without the other. As above, so below. In all things this balance exists.

The same is true of your relationship. In coming together with another human being, in a union of masculine and feminine, you are creating balance and harmony – generating life. The coming together of these two opposites creates a sacred, harmonious whole. You could even go so far as to say that no part of that harmonious whole can be fully satisfied until it is joined to the other.

This extends of course, to sexual union. This is the joining of the masculine and feminine (the blade and the vessel) in the physical plane – a magical, joyful, meaningful expression of love and harmony.

That is the mythological and allegorical context of creating a relationship. Connecting to the symbolism in myth and allegory deepens your connection to your partner and gives you a higher context for the relationship, beyond your everyday reality and the preoccupations of your limited self.

You are engaging your creative energy in generating harmony and balance, life-giving forces that will nourish not only yourself and your partner, but those around you as well.

Now Create It

That's it. You've discovered the dual nature of your being – your limited self and your boundless, infinite creative being. You know what you would truly love to create in a relationship. You have created a choice that will compel that relationship into reality.

Now go and create it. May your loving bring you great joy and satisfaction at every level of your being.

> *"Make the most of yourself, for that is all there is of you."*
>
> Ralph Waldo Emerson

PART 7

Resources

(i) Other Ways to Use this Book

I am assuming you have already read the book and are following your intuition to create the relationship of your dreams. If that's the case, read on. If not, read the rest of the book, otherwise you will only have part of the picture!

Refocusing

It is an inevitable fact of life that sometimes the power of your consciousness will be invested in your underlying assumptions. You will know that this is happening because your relationship will suffer, you will recognise old patterns and you may experience more conflict.

At these points, you can use this book intuitively to acknowledge what's going on for you and refocus on what you love. It's incredibly simple – just choose to serve your heart and ask what's going on for you and allow yourself to open the book to a page that will serve you. Be informed by what's on that page and take appropriate action.

Extend the Principles to Other Relationships

Everything I have presented in this book can be applied to your other relationships – with your family, friends, neighbours, work colleagues, etc.

Use the intuitive exercises to receive information about what you would love to create with these other people. Tune into a vision, current reality and action to take.

Use your intuition to tune into the true nature and expanded essence of any person you are close to or are having difficulties with. You will receive deeper insight by doing this, than you could ever receive by thinking about this person.

Use your imagination for everything in your life.

Apply it to Everything

Obviously this book is about relationships, but the model behind it, *It's All You*, can be applied to absolutely everything in your life: your job, your holiday, your dinner – anything that you want to create.

You can also view your life as a creation and apply the model, the premises, the revelation of underlying assumptions and the intuitive exercises to creating your life. You will be amazed and delighted not only by the transformation in yourself, but also by the changes in your circumstances.

Try it! Take an area in your life that you would love to transform and apply the principles in this book to it. Reveal your underlying assumptions, discover what you would truly love using the intuitive techniques and take action towards that. Notice the results in your life.

(ii) Soul Partner Guided Meditation

This meditation will powerfully connect you to what you would love to create in a relationship, whether it's a new relationship or transforming the one you already have. Be prepared to receive the wisdom of your divine creative being and then write it down. Be sure to capture the qualities and vibration of what you receive.

Sit comfortably and uncross your arms and legs. Take a few deep breaths and as you breathe out, relax into your body.

Begin to notice what is happening in you – what thoughts are passing through, what emotions you are experiencing, what sensations you are experiencing in your body. Allow them all to be there.

Now become aware of your heart space, that area at the centre of your chest. Breathe deeply into this space in your body and as you inhale, imagine the energy of your heart expanding. As you exhale, imagine your focus narrowing into your heart space.

Inhale – expand your heart energy.

Exhale – bring your focus deeper into your heart centre.

Keep inhaling and expanding and exhaling and focusing.

Now imagine as you inhale that your heart energy is expanding beyond your body. Imagine that energy expanding through your ribs, your spine and out through your clothes. Imagine it expanding until you are sitting in your heart energy.

Breathe deeply in this space – into the wisdom of your heart.

Now imagine you are beginning to move, to travel across time and space, held safely in your heart energy. Imagine this movement begins slowly. You are cradled in your heart energy beginning to travel across time and space.

Imagine leaving the earth and travelling out into the solar system. See the stars – keep expanding. Now imagine that you begin to travel faster. Imagine yourself cradled within your heart energy, streaking through space like a shooting star. Imagine the freedom and exhilaration of that.

Know that as you travel, your heart is taking you closer and closer to what you truly desire, bringing you nearer and nearer to the relationship you would love to create.

Keep imagining what it's like to travel through time and space cradled in your heart energy, approaching what your heart truly desires.

Imagine that your heart knows *exactly* where to go, that your heart will show you all the aspects of the relationship you would truly love to create.

Now imagine you are slowing down, coming gently back to land on earth. Waiting for you is your soul partner, another human being to share the journey with. Imagine landing, still within your heart energy next to another human. Greet this person with love and joy.

Now ask your heart, *"What is possible with my soul partner? Show me what I would truly love to create in my relationship."*

Allow images, sounds, scents and impressions to pour into your consciousness from your heart. Receive all that you would love to create. Revel in the vibration of your heart's desire.

Now begin to write what you have received, what your heart truly desires to create with this other being – your soul partner. Capture each element, knowing that as you write, more will come.

When you feel complete, gently return to normal consciousness, ready to create what you love.

(iii) Creator Alignment Process (modified)

Used with the kind permission of William Whitecloud (http://www.williamwhitecloud.com).

There is a shorter version of this process in the book (see page 59). This extended version is extremely useful when you are having relationship issues and are so clouded by your thoughts and emotions that you are unable to clearly see your truth. This may happen often in the beginning!

You can run through this process by yourself, but you will receive more from it if you ask someone else to run you through the questions. This allows you to focus solely on your responses.

The Creator Alignment is an intuitive process, so answer the questions automatically with whatever comes to you first – you have the answers within just waiting to be revealed. No thinking. Make sure you capture your answers on paper. Either write them down yourself or ask someone else to.

Be as brutally honest as you can. The more honest and truthful you are, the more you will receive from the process. When you tell the absolute ungarnished truth, you will learn an incredible amount about your assumptions, thoughts and emotions.

Before you begin, choose to receive the wisdom of your heart and request that the person asking the questions makes a choice to serve your heart.

Think of a current or recent conflict (problem) in your life

What's the problem?

What do you think about the problem?

How do you feel about the problem?

Definition and meaning

How are you defining your self?

How are you defining others?

How are you defining the world?

Think of an age in early childhood or early life

How old are you?

What are you experiencing?

If there is any tension in your body, breathe into that tension and ask, "What is this?"

In this early childhood experience, what are you deciding about yourself, others and life?

What is the underlying assumption created by that decision?

Where's the power? What do you make important? *(This is often a behaviour(s) or strategy.)*

What is the inevitable end result of that pre-occupation?

Healing the wound and reframing the problem as a Creator

Go back to the early life experience and bow down to the true nature and expanded essence of everyone involved, especially yourself.

How do you see the old experience from the standpoint of your true nature and expanded essence?

Bow down to your true nature and expanded essence now.

How do you see the current conflict from the standpoint of your true nature and expanded essence?

Step into innocence and choose to serve your heart. Define a circle around you as "what you would love in relation to all of this?" Ask for a symbol.

Interpret your symbol.

Define another circle around you as "what action (if any) is there to take towards what you would love?"

Receive the action to take (if any). Take that action!

(iv) Thoughts, Emotions and Assumptions

The following ten real-life examples of relationship problems and the accompanying thoughts, emotions and assumptions were revealed using the Creator Alignment Process (see page 197). When you read through, you will notice that the thoughts and emotions experienced do not always logically point to the underlying assumption. This is why using a process to find out your underlying assumptions is so helpful, you can be tricked by your thoughts and emotions!

In many cases, the assumption as defined by the respondent relates to the relationship issue, but is part of a broader underlying assumption that will affect much of the respondent's life (see first example below). The relationship issue was created by the power being with the respondent's assumption that they are not important to the masculine, but this is actually part of an underlying assumption that he/she is insignificant.

The assumption as defined by the respondent is a little like only seeing the feet of a pirate in the searchlight. To fully understand the dynamics that play out in your relationships, you want to see the whole pirate – eyepatch, blunderbuss, rum bottle and all! The underlying assumption will be responsible for many of the respondent's relationship issues, not just the one dealt with in the examples below.

1. Relationship problem
I want to be more open and expressive and intimate, but I'm not doing that.

Summary of thoughts
If I do that I'll be vulnerable; he'll never leave me alone.

I'm afraid I have created a reality I told others about.

Emotions experienced
Fear, anxiety.

Assumption as defined by respondent
I'm not important (to the masculine).

Underlying assumption
I'm insignificant.

—————————————————

2. Relationship problem
I don't feel financially supported by my partner.

Summary of thoughts
He's irresponsible, selfish, lazy.
I can't make any money myself.
I have to control finances, can't trust him.
There's never enough.

Emotions experienced
Uncertainty, anxiety, stress, hyper-vigilance, unsupported, drained.

Assumption as defined by respondent
I'm powerless.

Underlying assumption
I'm powerless.

———————————————

3. Relationship problem
I want to leave the relationship but can't.

Summary of thoughts
I have to wait longer; the right time will come.
It has to happen but maybe I'm wrong.
I need to be free.

Emotions experienced
Scared, vulnerable, excited, impatient, guilty.

Assumption as defined by respondent
I'm powerless and there's no point having my own desires.

Underlying assumption
I'm powerless.

———————————————

4. Relationship problem
I keep going out with women who are
geographically far away.

Summary of thoughts
Can I solve it? What should I do about it?
Round and round with thinking.
Maybe I can do something to fix it.
In the future it will be better.
It's too hard, don't even try.

Emotions experienced
Longing, excitement, despondency,
disappointment.

Assumption as defined by respondent
I'm unloveable/unwanted.

Underlying assumption
I'm unloveable.

———————————————

5. Relationship problem
I'm fighting with my partner.

Summary of thoughts
He's bad, he's unfair, it's unfair.
It's his fault not mine.
He's not giving me what I want, not

meeting my needs.

It's about me having control stuff, I make things a problem.

Emotions experienced
Angry, hurt like a little girl, sorry for myself.

Assumption as defined by respondent
I'm not important.

Underlying assumption
I'm insignificant.

————————————————

6. Relationship problem
My partner is in control of me

His drinking is (was) in control of me.

Summary of thoughts
It's frightening, dark; horrible pattern; might turn to violence.

Causes instability, turbulence and disappointment.

Causes hurt and pain.

Complete loss of control.

It creates chaos everyday.

Emotions experienced
Desperation, anger, dissatisfaction, fear, guilt, pure exhaustion, lots of adrenalin, stress.

Assumption as defined by respondent
I'm going to be let down.

Underlying assumption
I can't trust myself, others or the world.

––––––––––––––––––––

7. Relationship problem
My partner hasn't told his ex-wife he's seeing me.

Summary of thoughts
I want him to tell her because people are hassling me and telling me they're uncomfortable she doesn't know.

I think he may not be telling me the truth.

I imagine he's not going to work everyday – he's secretly seeing her – know it's nonsense.

She should know because it's not fair.

He'll never tell her.

Emotions experienced
Depressed, frustrated, sad, upset.

Assumption as defined by respondent
I don't trust others and they won't like me or love me.

Underlying assumption
I can't trust myself, others or the world.

––––––––––––––––––––

8. Relationship problem
My partner cut me off.

Summary of thoughts
I hate him, how dare he.

He doesn't deserve me, he's damaged.

He's not meant for me.

I don't want him or anyone.

I wasn't good enough.

Maybe she was thinner than me, more beautiful.

I became less attractive, I wasn't wealthy enough.

He started to notice the truth of me and didn't like it.

Emotions experienced
Fury, helpless, sad, desperate, shut down, bitter.

Assumption as defined by respondent
I can't make a right decision. I can't trust myself.

Underlying assumption
I can't trust myself, others or the world.

––––––––––––––––––

9. Relationship problem
I'm not happy with the way I've had to treat the other man.

Summary of thoughts

I should get over it.

Someone is stopping me from behaving how I would normally behave.

I'm being protected from myself.

Everyone is encouraging me to stay away.

No compassion.

Feels like I can't trust my intuition – it would be polluted.

It's cruel, it's making me hang on more, like he's died.

It's probably for the best but only a small part of me thinks that.

I must be a bit of a psycho, obsessive.

He would like to hear from me.

Emotions experienced

Bad – I've been bad, guilty, angry, powerless, unrequited sadness of something that didn't happen, depressed, uninspired.

Assumption as defined by respondent

What I love isn't mine.

Underlying assumption

I'm powerless.

––––––––––––––––––

10. Relationship problem

I keep hooking into pettiness in my relationship.

Summary of thoughts

He's too defensive.

It's me too.

Every day there's something. He finds fault with me. It pisses me off.

I think it's a strategy to keep me safe – not needing to go to depths.

It's messed up that we're so privileged.

It's pathetic, childish, I should know better.

I think it's dangerous to move beyond niggling at each other. We both do it to avoid intimacy.

Emotions experienced

Frustration, anger, rage, sadness, despair, numbness (avoiding feelings of passion and our sexuality).

Assumption as defined by respondent

It's not safe when I'm relating to men.

Underlying assumption

I can't trust myself, others or the world.

(v) Books

Campbell, Joseph. *Pathways to Bliss: Mythology and Personal Transformation*. Edited by David Kudler. New World Library, 2004.

Campbell, Joseph & Moyers, Bill. *The Power of Myth*. Edited by Betty Sue Flowers. Doubleday, 1988.

Campbell, Joseph. *The Hero with a Thousand Faces*. 1st edition, Bollingen Foundation, 1949. 2nd edition, Princeton University Press. 3rd edition, New World Library, 2008.

Fritz, Robert. *The Path of Least Resistance: Learning to Become the Creative Force in Your Own Life*. Ballantine Books, 1989.

Harpur, Patrick. *Mercurius: The marriage of heaven and earth*. Blue Angel Gallery, 2007.

Starbird, Margaret. *The Goddess in the Gospels: reclaiming the sacred feminine*. Bear & Co. Pub., 1998.

Three Initiates. *The Kybalion: The Hermetic Philosophy of Ancient Egypt and Greece.* 1st edition, Yogi Publication Society, 1912. 2nd edition, The Book Tree, 2004.

Whitecloud, William. *The Magician's Way: a story about what it really takes to find your treasure.* Wizdom Press, 2004. New World Library, 2010.

Trainings

Intuitive life coaching and readings:

http://www.pollyannadarling.com

Transformational training:

Australia and USA

http://www.williamwhitecloud.com

UK

http://www.darreneden.com